DIY Punk
As Education

A volume in
Critical Constructions: Studies on Education and Society
Curry Stephenson Malott, Brad J. Porfilio, Marc Pruyn, and Derek R. Ford
Series Editors

DIY Punk
As Education

From Mis-Education to Educative Healing

Rebekah Cordova
University of Florida

IAP

INFORMATION AGE PUBLISHING, INC.
Charlotte, NC • www.infoagepub.com

Library of Congress Cataloging-in-Publication Data

Names: Cordova, Rebekah.
Title: DIY Punk as education : from mis-education to educative healing / Rebekah Cordova.
Description: Charlotte, NC : Information Age Publishing, 2016. | Series: Critical constructions: studies on education and society | Includes bibliographical references.
Identifiers: LCCN 2016027720 (print) | LCCN 2016028610 (ebook) | ISBN 9781681235752 (pbk.) | ISBN 9781681235769 (hardcover) | ISBN 9781681235776
   (ebook) | ISBN 9781681235776 (EBook)
Subjects: LCSH: Learning. | Punk rock music. | Educational sociology.
Classification: LCC LB1060 .C66985 2016 (print) | LCC LB1060 (ebook) | DDC 370.15/23–dc23
LC record available at https://lccn.loc.gov/2016027720

Cover image by E. Bowers

Copyright © 2017 Information Age Publishing Inc.

All rights reserved. No part of this publication may be reproduced, stored in a retrieval system, or transmitted, in any form or by any means, electronic, mechanical, photocopying, microfilming, recording or otherwise, without written permission from the publisher.

Printed in the United States of America

Contents

Foreword xiii

Inspiration xvii

1 **Introduction** 1
    Punk Problem-Posing 3
    Public Pedagogy, Social Learning Theory, and Self-Directed
        Learning 5
        Public Pedagogy 6
        Social Learning Theory 9
        Self-Directed Learning 10
    Conclusion 12

2 **Punk As Education** 15
    Historical and Political Roots of Punk 16
    Hardcore Punk 18
    DIY (Do-It-Yourself) Ethic 19
    Punk Music Scene: Punk Shows and Lyrics 22
        Punk Shows 22
        Punk Lyrics: Straight Edge 24
        Punk Lyrics: Veganism/Vegetarianism 26
    Punk 'Zines 28
    Punk-Based Activist Organizations 31
        CrimethInc. Ex-Workers Collective 32
        Riot Grrrl! (1992–1996) 34
        Food Not Bombs (1980–Present) 36

v

Critique of Punk: Race and Whiteness 39
Collecting Stories 41
  The History and Aims of Phenomenology 41
  Punk Phenomenology 43
  Phenomenological In-Depth Interviewing 43
  Data Analysis: Interpretative Phenomenological Analysis (IPA) 44
  Limitations of Study 48

3 Punk Learner Narrative Profiles 51
Illustrated by E. Bowers
Narrative Profile Creation 52
Aaron 54
  Introduction 54
  Punk Learner Profile 55
Yam 62
  Introduction 62
  Punk Learner Profile 63
Sean 67
  Introduction 67
  Punk Learner Profile 68
Erin 72
  Introduction 72
  Punk Learner Profile 73
Dave 80
  Introduction 80
  Punk Learner Profile 81
Todd 87
  Introduction 87
  Punk Learner Profile 87

4 Punk and Education Horizons 95
Phenomenological Horizons 96
  Punk As: Learner Self-Concept Awareness 97
  Punk As: Miseducative Experience Awareness 101
  Punk As: Educative Healing 108
Conclusion 121

5 Discussion and Conclusion 123
Punk As: Public Pedagogy 124
Punk As Social Learning Theory 126
Punk As: Self-Directed Learning 127
Role of Miseducation 135
Role of Educative Healing 138
Summary and Future Research 144
Conclusion: A Desire Path 146

References 149
Additional Resources 161

List of Figures

Figure 1.1	Framework gears	13
Figure 3.1	Aaron at the blackboard	56
Figure 3.2	Preacher in the river	59
Figure 3.3	Aaron at the Hardback	60
Figure 3.4	Yam looking at maps	64
Figure 3.5	Yam and his wife	67
Figure 3.6	Sean imagining baseball	69
Figure 3.7	Sean looking at a test	70
Figure 3.8	Don't get bored	72
Figure 3.9	Erin as a young artist	74
Figure 3.10	Erin in school	77
Figure 3.11	Erin as grown punk artist	80
Figure 3.12	Dave as a young boy	82
Figure 3.13	Bad Religion cover	85
Figure 3.14	Todd in a tree	89
Figure 3.15	Todd listening to KUNV	90
Figure 3.16	We do our part	92

List of Tables

Table 1.1	Stages of Self-Directed Learning	11
Table 2.1	Interview Questions	49
Table 4.1	Phenomenological Horizons and Subthemes	98
Table 5.1	Public Pedagogy Evidence	126
Table 5.2	Social Learning Theory Evidence	128
Table 5.3	Self-Directed Learning Development Level Two Evidence	129
Table 5.4	Self-Directed Learning Development Level Three Evidence	130
Table 5.5	Self-Directed Learning Development Level Four Evidence	132
Table 5.6	Self-Directed Learning Commonalities Within Punk Engagement	133
Table 5.7	Self-Directed Learning Development Proposed Level Five Evidence	134
Table 5.8	Prepunk Miseducative Experiences	137
Table 5.9	Stages of Healing Evidence	140
Table 5.10	"Doer" As Healing Evidence	142
Table 5.11	Happiness As Healing Evidence	143
Table 5.12	Future Research in Educative Healing	146

Foreword

Contrary to popular (taught) belief, learning is not something that can be forced or controlled. A teacher vehemently tries to teach a child math. Meanwhile, the child is learning a great deal about the suppressed facial expressions of frustration, or about how to direct his/her attention away from someone speaking and out onto the world through a window. In this moment the child's eyes might be learning something about depth and distance, but it is not a process controlled or conducted by a teacher, in fact no one teaches you how to see and direct your eyes.

Learning is in essence self-directed by nature. But rather than harnessing children's natural ability to learn, we stifle it through the assumption that children must be forced to learn. We design schools for the very purpose of containing children in a gridlock where they can't escape, while force-feeding them information, and then we wonder why children are so reluctant to swallow and regurgitate what they are taught.

Fortunately, there is a part of human nature that cannot be contained, an almost anarchist yearning to express the potential that we instinctively know we have inside us. And however we try to dumb ourselves down, it cannot be repressed.

At all times during the course of human history there have been groups of people questioning the normative status quo of the current day and age. In ancient Greece, it was the cynics who abandoned material belongings and lived like dogs on the street. The 1960s had its beatniks, and in the

1980s a new group emerged, as a response to the rigidity and disparagement of the perhaps most dystopic time in human history.

Just like the cynics in ancient Greek, they were given a derogatory label with reference to being worthless criminals. But instead of taking offense, they embraced it and the role of being the black sheep in the dysfunctional human family, the one who carries the entire family's burdens on its sleeve, so that eventually someone will notice and see that something is very wrong, and actually do something about it.

Some years ago I was travelling with an impromptu circus consisting of a group of friends traveling from Freetown Christiania in Copenhagen, Denmark, to the Netherlands to be part of an alternative music festival outside of Amsterdam. On our way back through Northern Europe, we stopped at a solar driven anarchist community located in the heart of German punk culture; Kreuzberg, in Berlin. The tiny community was made up of around 20 caravans situated in a square formation with yards and small gardens in the center. Water was retrieved from an old pump in the middle of the community and electricity lasted as long as the sun would allow.

While we were there, the community had arranged a punk concert, and at some point during the concert I climbed on top of a huge speaker, to avoid the mosh pit and to get a better view. As the bass from the speaker was vibrating up through my body, I looked over the crowd of people dancing. There were pink and green Mohawks, military boots, piercings and metal studs, and then there were yards and yards of black fabric clinching to bodies revealing random pieces of flesh where the fabric had been torn.

It was a misty but warm summer evening; and as the band kept playing, the crowd was moshing into something that from up there looked like a wonderful chaotic embrace. It was as wild and unruly as it was harmonious and loving, just like self-directed learning often is. I thought to myself: this is freedom.

Punk is more than a youth phenomenon, more than angry social commentary expressed through erratic rock music. Punk is a purging of suppressed frustration with a society locked into paralyzing normativity, but it is also more than that. Punk has offered young people whose lives would otherwise have been destined for cultural captivity, the (relative) freedom to explore and experiment in a community operating on principles, but not laws.

As the young person steps through the doors into the punk community, he or she leaves behind the restraints of social class and enters a space where everyone is equal per definition, with music as its anchoring factor that brings everyone together.

Without the presence of adults preaching normative boundaries, the world is reset to its infant stages, to some—a wild and savage aspect of human nature. But it also means that the young people coming together in punk communities have the space to create a world of their own, and to question the status quo and powers that be in society. Vegan soup kitchens are established in the span of an afternoon, handmade tickets to underground concerts are written and dispersed efficiently in the hundreds, and fraction groups are mobilized when squatters' dwellings are threatened to form a public protest against the oppression of the establishment.

Unlike other emergent forms of youth culture expressed through music that questioned and challenged the status quo, punk was never made commercial and thereby its power was not pacified through it being immersed in popular culture.

Concurrently with the development of punk culture, a "new wave" of alternative education has been forming in the shadows of mainstream schooling, and just as punk culture challenges what we consider to be "taste" when it comes to music, clothing, and youth culture, this new wave of alternative education challenges our concepts of school and learning.

One of these punk forms of alternative education is unschooling, a concept coined by the late John Holt, which refers to a child being educated (or self-educated) outside of school, with no element of school being present in the child's educational process. There is thus no homework, no classes, and no teachers.

Described by unschooling advocate Ivan Illich, children (but also parents) transitioning from mainstream schooling to unschooling (or the related concepts world schooling, and life learning) will go through a "decompression" period that Illich called deschooling. This process involves unlearning the habits and patterns integrated into the child during his or her time in school, and often the child needs to "heal" from the experience of having been to school, which may involve a period of excessive over-indulgence in things that the child previously had been restricted from, such as "screen time" and sleep.

Most children eventually emerge from this process with the ability to make common sense decisions for their own life, finally being able to direct their own learning after spending most of their young life thrust in the arms of adults controlling every aspect of their day.

Punk has in many ways served a similar purpose in the lives of young adults who equally have been subject to the oppressing forces of adulthood and formal schooling. Punk has enabled children and young adults to create a space of their own where they could heal and find their own voice in a community based on strong humanitarian principles of freedom and compassion. Punk offers young adults the opportunity to learn and develop their skills in an environment where no one tells them what they can or cannot do. This means that they get to experiment and try out new (and sometimes outrageous) things, which contributes to raising their confidence and self-esteem.

That is how punk as a culture empowers young people to take life into their own hands, despite the lack of resources and formal forms of organization. Very few places in our society can say the same, least of all when it comes to empowering young people to discover their voice and their individual potential without limitation.

Rebekah Cordova underlines the connection between healing from the wounds inflicted upon us by a system of negligent oppression, and the power of self-directed learning spaces as she illustrates how important these spaces are in society, not only in punk communities, but in the sphere of education in general.

Drawing on the real and intimate voices of people identifying with the punk movement, Rebekah argues for the pedagogical leap forward needed for the spaces of education to start embracing the natural learning ability embodied by each child and the sovereignty thereof.

—**Anna Brix Thomsen**, MEd

Inspiration

BoySetsFire proceeded to play almost immediately. In a mere second, the entire room and stage exploded in energy; the chainlink fence that separates minors from drinkers shakes as people move along all areas of the floor, pressing hard against the platform stage. I stand completely mesmerized as the lead singer screams into the microphone.

> Resist
> It is a citizen's duty
> To resist the system
> That pits us against one another

The Raven, one of Denver's more formal venues for punk shows, exhudes excited fury after sheltering this first verse of the song "Prologue." I had just graduated high school a few months earlier and this show was one of the last local ones I was going to see before I went to college. BoySetsFire was not unique in their passionate connection to the practice of rebellion, but unlike other punk and hardcore bands of the 1990s, BoySetsFire spent little time on the hatred and blame of oppressive systems, but rather directs a call to action. BoySetsFire requires that you listen and move accordingly.

> Refuse
> It is a citizen's duty
> To refuse to believe the fears
> Their media has implanted

In us through sensationalized
And biased coverage.
Renounce
It is a citizen's duty
To renounce the idea of borders and boundaries
As they strengthen their hold on us
By serving the dual purpose
Of separating us
And therefore dividing our strength.

BoySetsFire unifies a group of nearly 100 kids at the Raven. I stand along the brick wall silent. Watching the fervor of the band and also the crowd; the pounding of the speakers guides the wave of hands and heads that move to the music. Then suddenly, BoySetsFire stops. The lead singer, Nathan Gray, is drenched in sweat as he takes off his shirt. BoySetsFire starts again. No spoken words to the audience as they try to catch their breath. The entire venue raises their fists in the air chanting along with Nathan.

Rise! Rise! Rise! Rise!
Rise! Rise! Rise! Rise!
Written signed off in the obituary what happened to us?
Where's your anger?
Where's your fucking rage?
Watered down senses lost

Every young person in the Raven knows these words; all at once, I realize how many people there are at the show. I can see the fence in the middle is starting to bend as it is not attached to anything but the ceiling; it sways back and forth violently.

Stand up!
Fight back!
How many starving millions have to die on our front doorsteps?
How many dying millions have to crawl to our front doorsteps?

All at once, I realize I have to move. Away from the swarming feel of the audience so that I can better see and hear the music. The crowd of kids starts to break up into smaller groups pushing and shoving one another. The power of the music is pulsating in each and every one of them—they move with and against the beat. I back up to the farthest corner of the section so as to keep my balance.

Where's your anger?
Where's your fucking rage?

> Watered down senses lost
> Unless we rise
> Tear it down
> Rise!

    The rage and anger are obvious in hardcore shows; there is rarely a lack of extreme emotion or physical interaction within the most politically charged songs. This last refrain of the song is Nathan's voice alone, but is quickly joined with the chorus of intense followers. Over and over I hear these words: "Rise! Rise!" Young people throughout the Raven move in unison with passion and dedication to his calling; to make change, to see the world for what it is, to fight for it to be something different, something better.

1

Introduction

> *When someone with the authority of a teacher, say, describes the world and you are not in it, there is a moment of psychic disequilibrium, as if you looked in the mirror and saw nothing.*
> —Adrienne Rich, 1986, p. 199

In her 1986 collection of prose, *Blood, Bread, and Poetry*, poet and activist Adrienne Rich discusses the complex nature of invisibility. Although Rich speaks candidly from a feminist lens, she is clear that invisibility is a painful condition, which one endures "when those who have power to name and to socially construct reality choose to not see or hear you" (Rich, 1986, p. 199), can apply to many people in numerous marginalized positionalities. To be a critical educator is to see that students, and young people in general, tend to be invisible in the schooling culture and structures. Whether it is because they are being schooled rather than educated (Gatto, 2003, 2005; Hern, 2008; Holt, 1989; Illich, 1971) or because their cultural identity, language, or lived story is not represented in the standards-based curriculum (Gay, 2000; Ladson-Billings, 1994, 1995; Knauss, 2009; Nieto, 1994; Nieto & Bode, 2007), young people struggle to locate themselves within empowering school environments that authentically acknowledge their complex identity and voice (Fine & Weiss, 2003; Lawrence-Lightfoot, 2004).

As a former classroom teacher working within a spectrum of settings, from traditional district schools to experiential charter schools, as well as residential treatment centers and juvenile detention settings, I became intimately aware of how invisible young people were within our schools. This experience of invisibility, which was manifested not only in the ways student voice and agency was diminished, but also through the controlling of their physical movements, was especially strong for those who rebelled against the mainstream school culture of obedience through forms of resistance.

Perhaps sadly ironically, since much of the structures and logistics of schooling are built to erase or control student agency, the subject of student engagement is a consistent topic of professional development and discussion within the education profession. We know, as teachers, that learning cannot occur without active and free student participation, but authentic whole student ownership over their learning is constantly constrained by the norms and conditions of our systems; the solutions remain elusive to us.

In my own attempt to seek pedogogical inspiration to increase engagement, I stumbled upon Kahn-Egan's (1998) "Pedagogy of the Pissed: Punk Pedagogy in the First-Year Writing Classroom," and it quickly transformed the way I saw curriculum and instruction in the classroom. This article, although nearly a decade old when I first read it, was the first academic work in which I saw concepts of punk culture in the ways I had lived it combined with the art of teaching in order to reach a more enthused and vivrant classroom ecology. Kahn-Egan starts by describing how common instructional practices aimed to create educational experiences that empower students or make them more visible, actually cultivate passivity in students because they leave classrooms with little sense of responsibility to their own educational pursuits. These practices, which seek to empower students, often focus on merely including them in the dominant cultural discourse of the classroom or school (often described as "giving student's voice") and actually do little to address the issue of student invisibility and largely just reaffirm the dominant status of specific race, class, age, and gender in the educational system.

As a response to learner passivity and disinterest, Kahn-Egan explores what it might mean to authentically engage students through the use of what he describes as a punk pedagogy. It is through the use of punk pedagogy in a classroom that students learn to be "critical of themselves, their cultures, and their government... of institutions in general," and most importantly, they go beyond merely criticizing, but also evaluate how to use their identity and voice to impact their community (Kahn-Egan, 1998, p. 100).

Inspired by Kahn-Egan's words and descriptions of the possibilities of punk informing my work as a teacher, I continued to explore what this could mean not only for my own practice, but for the education profession at large. As I pursued punk pedagogy in my research and with students, I started to consider that punk pedagogy, as a practice, has deep unexplored connections to its source: punk rock. If a punk pedagogy could advance the educative experiences in the traditionally oppressive classroom, I imagined that it was because there were already educative experiences at play, a curriculum of sorts, at work within the punk communities outside of schools.

On an experiential level I knew this pedagogy, or punk curricula, existed in some form; it was my own involvement in 1990s hardcore punk and the straight edge movement (a drug-free subset of punk) that led me to make significant dietary and political decisions based on punk cultural norms and knowledge that I had gathered and internalized. My own experiences were not in isolation; often I would hear from community members that their participation in punk was a transformative experience. Punk offered them voice and affirmation in a community; they were seen and heard in ways they had never been before.

Perhaps because I was starting to pay more attention to these connections, I began noticing narrative patterns emerge in columns within punk magazines that illustrated a more explicit connection between punk participation and education. Most notably, a specific column in the punk 'zine *Maximum Rocknroll* became the catalyst for my research, and ultimately, this book:

> I always tell people that punk rock was my education, my real high school.
> (*Maximum Rocknroll*, #326, 2010, p. 6)

Reading these words had a visceral impact on me—The naming of school (as something other than the stereotypical brick building down the street) was a bold and empowered step for this reader: He owed his education to punk rock.

Punk Problem-Posing

> *Because my academic discipline is education,*
> *my work as a scholar and theoretician is structured pedagogically.*
> —Pinar, 2012, p. 1

> *The functional role of punk subculture is to exist outside the main culture,*
> *while illuminating the central features of it.*
> —Levine & Stumpf, 1983, p. 433

As an education scholar seeking to understand the ways punk engagement could make any difference in the dismissive culture of schooling, I first attempted to consider the philosophical threads and tensions at hand. What does punk engagement offer education theory or pedagogy? If I am to believe that schooling is, by nature, oppressive, then in what ways can tenets of punk address this issue? How can punk help us reimagine educative spaces? My initial response was to parallel my questions, alongside the *Maximum Rocknroll* narrative, within a *problem-posing* framework.

Critical education scholar Joan Wink describes the power of Freire's (1970) problem-posing within education research:

> Problem posing ignites praxis and leads to action. Problem posing brings interactive participation and critical inquiry into the existing curriculum and expands it to reflect the curriculum of the students' lives. (Wink, 2005, p. 51)

For me, it is this acknowledgment of the "curriculum of the students' lives" that is at the heart of understanding the nature of engaged learning, which is key in being seen and visible in an educational setting. Given this, I resolved that the reflective narrative written in *Maximum Rocknroll* (2010) acted as an initial footing for further exploration as it put forth the clear and unmistaken lived reality that there exists contexts where learners access (or create) an environment that they perceive as meeting the aims of schooling if school, itself, disappoints. In short, by reporting that punk had acted as a "real high school," there exists a curriculum of life to elucidate. As I furthered my understand of a punk pedagogy, I pondered: If we can better understand the ways in which learners make empowered choices to engage in self-determined sites of learning, then perhaps we can work to improve the levels of engagement within all realms of education systems in which we find ourselves invested.

Clearly, as an educator and a student of education, I knew that the efforts to identify and understand how and when young people learn outside of formal classroom instruction was not new (see Dewey, 1938/1997; Eisner, 1994; Fine, 1991; Schubert, 1981; Vygotsky, 1978); my exploration would fit in among a very large spectrum of curriculum and education scholars. As one point of specification, having written on the topic of curriculum for decades, Schubert continues to advocate for increased study of outside curriculum in such realms of "life as families, homes, peer groups, nonschool organizations, communities, and mass media" (Schubert, 2010, p. 71). Additionally, Pinar, discusses his reflective method of *currere*, where the study of curriculum is not contained within formal school walls, rather it is defined as "complicated conversation" where curriculum is best understood through self-reflection, subjectivity, and an analysis of lived experience (Pinar, 2012, p. 6). Similar sentiments exist within a younger generation of scholars who breathe new life into the academic discipline of education through their work to showcase the curriculum of educative experiences away from school: Morrell and Duncan-Andrade (2002), Emdin (2010), Hill (2007, 2009), and Hill and Petchauer (2013) discuss the ways in which hip-hop plays a key role in the advancement of literacy and other content areas; Soep and Chavez (2010) showcase sites of learning within youth radio media creation; while Hern (2008) discusses the multiple opportunities for youth to become educated through de-schooling projects within their own communities. These works are but a small sample of the ways in which educators are responding to the request for "increased efforts by researchers, activists, artists, and practitioners to take up questions around education that exist outside of institutional purview" and "to reevaluate some of the disciplinary boundaries that define the field" (Sandlin, O'Malley, & Burdick, 2010, p. 363).

In essence, classic and contemporary education scholars assert that there is much to be learned from the chosen endeavors of students outside of the school setting and that the formal curriculum may be best influenced by the informal curriculum chosen by youth when they are able to find empowered spaces of learning of their own. Thus, expanding out from my initial interest in Kahn-Egan's punk pedagogy to include punk participation and the connection to education, my problem-posing led me to these questions:

- What is the experience of adults who conceptualize their engagement with punk as educative?
- What role punk plays in learner self-confidence?
- What might punk engagement teach educators about perceptions of educative experiences?

In my pursuit to make meaning of these questions within my lived experience and the lived experiences of others, I turned to the public pedagogy, social learning theory, and self-directed learning disciplines.

Public Pedagogy, Social Learning Theory, and Self-Directed Learning

Humans seem to learn more deeply, and more equitably, without gaps between rich and poor, when they learn outside of school in areas they choose and for which they are motivated.
—Hayes & Gee, 2010, p. 185

As Hayes and Gee articulate, I believe that the most intuitively fitting environments for learning may not exist within our current form of schooling; rather, they likely sit within the contexts of lived experience outside of school. My aim, through this book, is to contribute to scholarship that integrates learning contexts from the margins of education rhetoric and move it into the center of analysis by better understanding, and to uncover the essence of the learning experience outside of school specifically within the chosen subculture of punk. To do this in both a broad and deep way, I continually reference and ground the work in the theoretical combination of public pedagogy as defined by Giroux (1988, 2004a, 2004b) and Sandlin, Schultz and Burdick (2010); social learning theory by Vygotsky (1978); and self-directed learner development by Grow (1991).

Public Pedagogy

> *Education is an enveloping concept, a dimension of culture that maintains dominant practices while also offering spaces for their critique and re-imagination.*
> —Sandlin, Schultz, & Burdick, 2010, p. 1

> *Education in every country and in every epoch has always been social in nature. Indeed, by its very essence it could hardly exist as anti-social in any way . . . it was never the teacher or the tutor who did the teaching, but the particular social environment.*
> —Vygotsky, 1997, p. 47

Giroux reminds us that "pedagogy is not simply about the social construction of knowledge, values, and experiences; it is also a performative practice embodied in the lived interactions among educators, audiences, texts, and institutional formations" (Giroux, 2004a, p. 61). As such, the study of public pedagogy is the accounting of ways in which multiple discourses function as an educational force to bridge the "gap between private and public discourses, while simultaneously putting into play particular ideologies and values that resonate with broader public conversations regarding how society views itself and the world of power, events, and politics" (Giroux, 2009, p. 12). Within this context of public pedagogy, there exist cultural texts and forms of curriculum, which contribute to this broader conversation and inform the actions and behaviors of participant learners.

For many readers new to the education discipline, the term curriculum might seem out of place when referring to experiences outside the formal classroom setting; however, curriculum outside of the school walls has long been discussed by education scholars. In the United States context of the Common School Movement during the mid-1800s, what was considered to be educative and worthy of formal instruction (as opposed to within the realm of the "family") was not only a topic of impassioned debate, but often acted as a foundational, albeit radical, guiding question (Mann, 1840/1989; Rury, 2005). The societal response to these wonderings were instrumental in the creation of our schooling system; however, discussions of what is worth teaching and learning have never ceased. Jerome Bruner describes this ever cyclical process of seeking clarity on curriculum as "an animated conversation on a topic that can never be fully defined" (Bruner, 1996, p. 116).

I imagine contemporary public pedagogy scholars draw from Cortes (1979, 1981), where, in some of his earliest work, he discussed "societal curriculum" as the "massive, ongoing, informal curriculum of family, peer groups, neighborhoods, mass media, and other socializing forces that educate" (Cortes, 1979, p. 475). Elliot Eisner (1994) further complicates the notion of curriculum when he claims that it falls into three categories: the *explicit*, the *implicit*, and the *null*. The explicit curriculum focuses on the overt and formal instruction, while the implicit and null curriculum capture unspoken norms and (de)valuation of academic content. Eisner's three categories, although largely used to analyze formal schooling, can easily be used to make meaning of any learning context and further pushes on any type of concrete vision of how curriculum operates. Marsh and Willis (2003), in *Curriculum: Alternative Approaches, Ongoing Issues*, discuss additional varied forms of curriculum, making specific note of the types that are most useful for living in a chosen society, and build skills for questioning authority and searching for understanding.

Schubert (1981, 2010) argues clearly for the possibilities of engaging specific curriculum categories and frameworks to interpret "out-of-school curriculum." According to Schubert, these "outside areas" explicitly or implicitly harbor a curriculum of intentions, hidden messages, null or neglected offerings, overt and covert teachings, formal or informal tests and evaluations, lived experiences, and embodiments of meaning (as cited in Burdick, Sandlin & O'Malley, 2013). Additionally, Philip Jackson (1968/1990) is credited with introducing the notion of *hidden curriculum*, in his book *Life in Classrooms*, which is described as the values, dispositions, and social and behavioral expectations that brought rewards in school for students.

In a response to these explorations through the varied applications and locations of curriculum, public pedagogy seeks to understand sites of education that transcend "the school to a host of other institutions that educate: families, churches, libraries, museums, publishers, benevolent societies, youth groups, agricultural fairs, radio networks, military organizations, and research institutes" (Cremin, 1976, p. xi). In addition, nontangible experiences and collective notions of learning, such as sites of activism, public intellectualism, and grassroots social movements, are considered public pedagogy as they are linked to experiences that educate and empower (Cortes, 1981; Sandlin, Schultz, & Burdick, 2010). In essence, public pedagogy aims to shine a very bright light on the curriculum in which young people engage daily throughout their lives, so as to define education and learning in significantly expanded ways than typically described in traditional education rhetoric.

Current scholarship in public pedagogy has begun to carve out a firm place within the curriculum studies field, as education theorists continually make sense of the nature of learning beyond what has been conceived in the formal school setting. Schubert likens the study of public pedagogy to John Dewey's notion of collateral learning, which highlights the fact that students "learn much in addition to or apart from that which educators intend" (Schubert, 2010, p. 12), and that often schools can be "miseducative," whereas experiences outside of school can be far more "educative" (p. 11). Additionally, William Pinar affirms the crucial importance of prioritizing the field of public pedagogy as a separate discipline within curriculum studies because it is clear that:

> Education now occurs everywhere, *but* inside the school...school de-form has expelled pedagogy from schools, evidently into the streets (including parades), onto television, into the movies, on the Internet, through music (and not only hip-hop), poetry and the visual arts (including graffiti), in museums, on bodies, and at the zoo. It is as if the world has somehow become a "safe haven" where, paroled from the "prison" of the school-as-institution, we can (finally) teach. (Pinar, 2010a, p. xv)

The punk community is largely based on the performance of one of many forms of punk ideology, being, and learning; while punk fits well in the public pedagogy frame. In essence, there is learning that occurs while engaged in punk, and this learning can be conceptualized and articulated through multiple space descriptors within public pedagogy. This idea can be further understood through the education theories of educative spaces. For instance, in their piece "Public Pedagogy through Video Games: Design, Resources & Affinity Spaces," Hayes and Gee (2009) might describe punk shows or 'zines as *affinity spaces* where learners utilize or create "well-designed spaces that resource and mentor learners, old and new, beginners and masters alike" (p. 185), or as a *free space*, defined by Polletta as "small-scale settings within a community or movement that are removed from the direct control of dominant groups, are voluntarily participated in, and generate the cultural challenge that precedes or accompanies political mobilization" (Polletta, 1999, p. 1). Finally, punk might be defined as a *transitional space* that Ellsworth refers to as "the kinds of educational environments that facilitate new, creative, spontaneous ways of learning and of seeing the self in relation to others" (Ellsworth, 2005, p. 258).

To conclude, the area of public pedagogy expands our current notions of what education looks like and the space it can occupy; both constructs have tremendous implications for schooling and nonschool settings.

> These are public pedagogies—spaces, sites, and languages of education and learning that exist outside of the walls of the institution of schools... they are just as crucial—if not more so—to our understanding of the developments of identities and social formations as the teaching that goes on within the classroom. (Sandlin, Schultz, & Burdick, 2010, p. 1)

Social Learning Theory

> *I think the early political hands helped set the tone... once I was engaged and conscious of this political world, I felt others in the scene were as well and I could talk with them. It was a real community in the sense of shared values/ideals, and I definitely didn't feel that from my family or school.*
> —Angel, as cited in Peterson (2009, p. 13)

In education scholars' desire to understand the way learners make meaning from educative experiences, educators turn to explicating ways in which the act of learning occurs. Although there are several available for consideration, Lev Vygotsky's social learning theory is the most appropriate for this book as it assumes:

- learners are prone to learn through the imitation of models and examples of activism and behavior they see in social scenarios;
- learners can quickly decode the behavior/consequence relationship for learner behavior, belief, and actions; and
- learning happens before and after physical/intellectual development, they are interconnected at all levels (Vygotsky, 1978).

Vygotskty imagined learning occurring through the intersections of social interaction and language. Learning was the (inter)action that:

> Calls to life in the child, awakens and puts in motion an entire series of internal processes of development. These processes are at the time possible only in the *sphere of interaction* with those surrounding the child and in collaboration with companions, but in the internal course of development, they eventually become the internal property of the child (Vygotsky, as cited in Wertsch, 1985, p. 71)

The "sphere" mentioned refers to the zone of proximal development (ZPD) where learning and development are entwined, dragging and pulling at one another to reach a new level of ability and confidence; learning and development were best understood together as a whole concept, not apart. In *Mind and Society*, Vygotsky defines the ZPD as "the distance between the actual developmental level as determined by independent problem solving and the level of potential development as determined through problem solving under adult guidance or in collaboration with more capable peers" (Vygotsky, 1978, p. 86). In essence, learners reside within zones that give name to the space between who they are, how they perform, and who they are becoming, thus movement between these zones allows them to always become new.

As an integral part of the ZPD framework, the more knowledgeable other (MKO) is a necessary coach in the learning and social development process. Vygotsky (1978) describes an MKO as defined as those who are to teach. Traditionally, and in the school classroom, it is assumed that the MKO is an adult teacher; however, within current education theory, the MKO could most likely be a peer, a younger person, or organized effort (Wertsch, 1981). In this research, I imagine social learning theory (specifically with a focus on the ZPD and the MKO) to be instrumental in providing a space to honor the essence of learning within punk engagement; discovering where the MKO or ZPD reside in the punk learning process is of primary interest to understanding the essence of a learning experience. As Vygotsky articulated, "it is through others that we develop into ourselves" (p. 161).

Self-Directed Learning

*Education should produce self-directed, lifelong learners,
but sometimes it creates dependency instead.*
—Gerald Grow, 1991, p. 127

Social learning theory and public pedagogy actualized within the punk community can be well understood by considering the DIY (do-it-yourself) punk ethos, described by Moran (2011), as "one of the most important factors fueling the subculture... which kept the punk subculture alive since the late 1970s" (p. 1), and its impact on learning. As a fitting framework to explore independent or DIY learning, I use Grow's (1991) self-directed learner development (SDL) rubric as way to explore the DIY learning spectrum within punk experiences and community engagement.

Grow (1991) was inspired to create a model of self-directed learner development after teaching college-level classes to adults whom he imagined would exhibit high levels of independence in the classroom contexts, compared to that of younger students. What he found instead was that adults, like children, performed in a teacher-dependent manner. With this in mind, he proposed that self-direction should be the goal of schools and other educational organizations in order to fight against the "dependency" that was often the unfortunate outcome of schooling systems and structures (p. 127). As a contribution to what he saw as an increasingly dire issue in education, Grow asserted that self-direction could be taught, or at least measured along a spectrum, in hopes that while content mastery was evaluated, actual self-directed learner qualities could also be assessed and enhanced. Grow proposed using a simple rubric model (Table 1.1) to understand where learners were along there journey of self-direction (p. 129):

In Stage 1, the dependent learner is most receptive to explicit and directed instruction. Clear ideas of what is considered "correct" or "incorrect" are important components of this direct instruction, as well as immediate feedback on student production. In Stage 1, the learning environment is teacher-centered, with the teacher having all the knowledge and the student acting as a passive learner. Freire (1970) discusses a similar concept of dependency in his description of the *banking method* of instruction, where teachers make "deposits" into students as they sit and wait for imparted knowledge with no active engagement or meaning making; Fox also describes this pedagogy as *transfer theory:*

> People who adopt the transfer theory of teaching see knowledge as a commodity, which can be transferred, by the act of teaching, from one container to another or from one location to another. Such people tend to express their view of teaching as "imparting knowledge" or "conveying information." (Fox, 1983, p. 152)

Stage 2 learners are considered interested and available for learning—they show some signs of independence after the teacher showcases the reasoning behind the instruction; these learners require consistent

TABLE 1.1 Stages of Self-Directed Learning

Stage	Student	Teacher/Experience	Examples
Stage 1	Dependent	Authority	Coaching types of instruction with immediate feedback.
Stage 2	Interested	Motivator, Guide	Inspired lecture with guided discussion. Goal setting and learning strategies.
Stage 3	Involved	Facilitator	Discussion facilitated by teacher who participates as equal.
Stage 4	Self-Directed	Consultant	Engaged work, individual projects

encouragement and external motivators in order to stay confident in their ability to create or produce. Stage 2 learning is most conducive within a close relationship between student and learner where the teacher uses charisma to incite excitement in the student, as well as make connections between the learning objective and the student's interests.

Grow points out that Stage 2 is often the beginning and end of where most teachers who are considered "highly-effective" sit; unfortunately, Stage 2, unless it is clearly moving toward Stage 3, is still asking the student to be dependent on the teacher to give praise and make important connections before the student can move forward independently. As schools are based on the compliance of students to adhere to school systems (Dewey, 1938/1997; Eisner, 1994; Holt, 1964, 1976; Kohl, 1991; Postman, 1995; Postman & Weingartner, 1971) regulations, norms, and procedures, Stage 2 learning is typically at the peak of independent experiences that the most progressive of school cultures allow for.

Stage 3 learners are defined as involved and see themselves as participants in their own education as they don't require external motivation or praise to seek engagement in learning; they also "develop critical thinking, individual initiative, and a sense of themselves as co-creators of the culture that shapes them. This may involve a therapy-like shift of personal paradigm" (Grow, 1991, p. 133). In Stage 3, the teacher or learning experience acts as a guide, rather than an authority or gatekeeper of knowledge. In schools, teachers who align with critical pedagogy (McLaren, 2014; Shor, 1987, 1996; Wink, 2005) or certain aspects of education humanism (Huitt, 2001) best actualize Stage 3 in their classroom when they focus on peer-group projects as well as student-centered/student-led curriculum and instruction. Stage 4, the last stage in Grow's rubric, is described as the mature or high self-directed stage where learners are so completely aware of their learning ability and skills that they can learn from any kind of teacher or experience, but thrive in contexts of autonomy and independence (p. 134). Interestingly, Grow asserts that "fully self-directed learning is not possible in an institutional setting" despite the notion that self-directed learning should be offered as the "single most important outcome of formal education" (Grow, 1991, p. 135).

Conclusion

Public pedagogy, social learning theory, and self-directed learning development are the guides I use to uncover the nuances of the educative experience that reside within punk engagement. To best illustrate this framework set and the ways in which they each fit within an appropriate analytical structure, I put forth an image of gears (Figure 1.1) rotating to

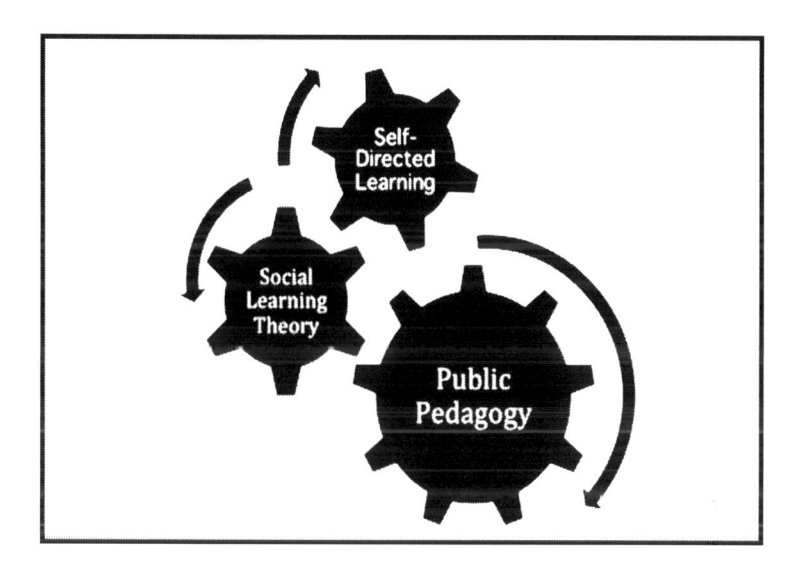

Figure 1.1 Framework gears.

form the interplay between the frameworks that ultimately creates a learning environment.

At a theoretical and pedagogical level, there exists the goals and aims of public pedagogy, specifically regarding democracy as defined by Giroux (2004, 2006). These pedagogical movements and atmospheres are found in numerous settings and ecologies; they provide the theoretical context for the interactions to exist within. These specific interactions can be imagined and analyzed through social learning theory; specifically as it connects to the meaning of language and interpersonal communications between those who are defined as the learner and those that may act as a teacher. These educative interactions will lead the learner to exhibit behaviors that can be plotted within a development rubric of self-directed learning (Grow, 1991), in an effort to reach the ultimate goal of independent actualized learning. Each of these three frameworks not only operates in its own way, but acts in accordance with the others to provide an overarching atmosphere to unpack educative moments, both short and long, that fall along the learner journey.

The following chapters in this book detail an attempt to see and understand the educative experiences of those within the punk community, and in doing so, hold space for these storied experiences within a greater conversation framed by the above theoretical constructs. Chapter 1 outlines the research position, research problem-posing, as well as the theoretical framework that assists in framing these stories. Chapter 2 discusses the scholarship and insider writing that paints the historical and contemporary landscape of punk ideology as it relates to learner identity and educative engagement. This chapter also offers a detailed description of the phenomenological in-depth interviewing process used throughout the research, as well the rationale for choosing interpretive phenomenological analysis (IPA) as the method for analyzing the narratives.

Chapter 3 contains six author constructed narratives, created using text from interview transcriptions, meant to represent the educative path each punk learner traveled on before and during their punk engagement. Chapter 4 is a thorough exploration of the phenomenological horizons that emerged through detailed narrative data coding using interpretive phenomenological analysis (IPA) processes. These horizons articulate one set of meanings that can be made from the narratives collected in the research process. Chapter 5 offers an advanced analysis of the phenomenological horizons through the framework set articulated in Chapter 1, as well as reccomendations for further research.

2

Punk As Education

In order to best articulate the nature of punk rock, it is important to note that the spirit of the movement is hard pressed to be clearly defined or analyzed. Punk, in all of its facets, has evolved over several decades and across several political geographical borders. According to sociologist Ross Haenfler:

> It becomes more difficult to speak of "punk" except as an umbrella identity encompassing the variety of punk influenced genres that fragmented from the original incarnation: gutter punk, emo, hardcore, straight edge, screamo, anarchist punk, pop punk, goth punk, post punk. The process continues as fragments break up even further—sXe [straight edge] emerged from hardcore, itself a fragment of punk. Each subgroup becomes more particularistic, more specialized, and often believes it is more true to the original spirit of the movement. (Haenfler, 2006, p. 198)

Punk's impact is not easily captured in one field of scholarship; it is found spread amongst sociology (Beer, 2014; Bennett, 2006; Hebdige, 1995; Moore & Roberts, 2009), English (Kahn-Egan, 1998; One, 2005; Sirc, 1997; Traber, 2001, 2007), women's studies (Reddington, 2007; Roman, 1987) music theory (Dale, 2012; Ware, et al., 2014), cultural studies (Moore, 2007; Sabin, 1999), history (Shahan, 2013), political science (Ardizonne, 2005; Malott & Pena, 2004; O'Connor, 2003), and even international relations (Dunn, 2008). Despite the seemingly clear connection between punk participation and DIY (do-it-yourself) learning (as articulated by classroom teachers [see Barlic, 2014; Coles, 2014; Johnson, 2011]), I could not find any distinct research within the education discipline addressing punk specifically through curricular, instructional, or learning theory frames. Acknowledging this apparent gap in education scholarship, I outline in the following chapter a specific selection of written works where punk community and ideology is linked to the lived educative experience of punk participants, even if they are not overtly describing their engagement using education terminology.

Nearly every written work on punk begins by describing how indescribable punk is and how difficult it is to pinpoint the exact beginnings of the music or cultural movement; however, if one is to attempt to conceptualize punk rock, the roots of the social movement are an important place to start. In the following pages, I highlight the political roots of punk, as well as the subsequent evolution of *waves* within the culture. The bulk of the chapter focuses on Hardcore punk and the aspects that connect to my research, specifically DIY ethics, punk 'zines, and punk activist organizations. As there are limited scholarly works focusing on punk, I include works self-published by punk experts who are insiders to punk who may or may not be part of an academic scholar community. In the pages that follow, my intention is to show that punk, in terms of its connection to education, learning theory, and curriculum studies, is a rather unexplored area of research within a larger body of (sub)cultural and political critique. Please note that the following detail is not meant to be an exhaustive timeline of the history of punk, but rather a brief description of the punk cultural and historical markers that assist us in perceiving it through a curricular lens.

Historical and Political Roots of Punk

Although the exact root of punk rock has been debated, many punks and punk movement scholars trace punk to the mid-1970s in England. Bands such as the Sex Pistols and Crass seem to inhabit the space reserved for the beginning of punk music and the punk scene as set in England's working-class struggle. Many of the lyrics associated with punk music in the late-1970s London reference the plight and angst of those who were young, White, male, poor, and unemployed (Dancis, 1978; Laing, 1978). Given this environmental imprint, the individual's personal/political relationship has long been at the foundation of the punk music movement.

Davies (1996), categorizes English punk into two political waves: first wave (1976–1978) and second wave (1978–1982). With the rise of Conservative Party member Enoch Powell and the appointment of Margaret Thatcher as the Secretary of State for Education and Science, the early 1970s in England marked the beginning of a political climate that birthed the first wave of punk music. England was faced with increasing fascist movements in the form of the National Front political party and a deepening of the racist offensive against Black and immigrant workers by the government (Hearse, 1997). Thatcher, facing tremendous racial and class divides within England, used her campaign platform as a way to unite White English citizens against those who were to blame for the poor economy. Those communities targeted included, but weren't limited to, Pakistanis, Jews, North Africans, and Afro-Caribbeans.

Attempting to capitalize on punk as a youth connector and motivator, the National Front (NF), Britain's longest-lived White Nationalist political movement, began supporting the fascist components of punk. The NF focused on the punk bands (e.g., Skrewdriver, Adam Ant and the Ants) within England that seemingly supported the mission and goals of NF (namely the end of protected immigration in England). However, in these early years, the majority of bands within the first wave of punk's reaction was less about uniting against the government or about demonized immigrants, rather it was "the quintessential rebellion, [as] punk was based on doing the opposite of what is expected...its point is subversion, rather than critique" (Davies, 1996, p. 14). First wave punks found joy in their alienation and gained empowerment through their class-based marginalization; they glorified the destruction of the normed society more than they were invested in societal change.

First wave punk came to the United States in the early-1970s; however, the highly individualistic and materialistic nature of U.S. society altered the drive and agenda of punk. Instead of being fueled by economic despair, punk in the United States was more about general individual rebellion, non-conformity, and artistic expression. Bands such as the Ramones, the Germs, the Subhumans, and Iggy Pop played specific venues in New York City to promote the underground music and art scene; by the late-1970s, punk music, and its growing affiliation with an aesthetic style (see Fox, 1987; Ward, 1996) had spread to both coasts.

The second wave of punk shifted punk's cultural impact on Britain, marking a clear departure from individualistic lyrics signifying hopelessness, moved toward a call to action. Bands such as Stiff Little Fingers (Ireland) and The Clash (England), gained popularity in the United States with their song lyrics primarily calling for unification and personal accountability as a response to oppression. According to Dave Laing, one of the earliest British academics to explore punk as a political movement, the bands of the British Second wave sought to energize and inspire their audience, a strategy that was markedly different than the first wave whose aims were to primarily to give voice to desperation and frustration. At this time in England, the late 1970s to the early 1980s, organized movements against the fascist National Front were largely supported by punks, and many bands were actively engaged in antiracist events and campaigns:

> That [punk] hostility took three major forms: a challenge to the "capital-intensive" production of music within the orbit of the multi-nationals, a rejection of the ideology of "artistic excellence," which was influential among established musicians, and the aggressive injection of new subject-matter into popular song, much of which (including politics) had previously been taboo. (Laing, 1978, p. 124)

Hardcore Punk

In the United States, second wave punk (this can be generally conceived during the years 1978–1983) was marked with the evolution into hardcore punk, with the bands Bad Brains, Teen Idles, Untouchables, Minor Threat, and The Faith from Washington, DC (Kuhn, 2010). This new wave attempted to solidify punk as a youth-driven political statement. Hardcore swept away much of the isolated and nihillistic attitudes that had come with the first wave and built upon the cultural and economic critique of the British second wave; hardcore ushered in the notion of community, responsibility, and social justice activism.

> [T]he defeat and retrenchment of previous Left social movements created a vacuum for punk- inspired protest to emerge with new mobilizing structures, frames of meaning, collective identities, and tactical repertoires. In the case studies we discuss, punks brought these novel means of protest into ongoing struggles against racism, the nuclear arms race and U.S. imperialism, and sexism. (Moore & Roberts, 2009, p. 276)

Predominately in the large urban centers of the East and West coasts of the United States, (Washington, DC; Boston; New York City; and Los Angeles), hardcore also found its way into smaller cities; Denver and Salt Lake City were hubs in the West, while Gainesville, Florida, became a hub for the South.

Published works focusing on hardcore punk culture and community include several recent academic articles focusing on engagement with hardcore music (Attfield, 2011; Goshert, 2000; Hancock & Lorr 2012), gender politics and identity (Ensminger, 2010; Griffin, 2012; Purchla, 2011), race and ethnicity (Fiscella, 2012; Traber, 2001), as well as what is considered *insider* (i.e., those who are/were participants in punk) works written by punks about their experience and participation in punk. A few of the most cited volumes written by insiders include a self-published punk manifesto (which was so sought after by readers that the author had to sign a publishing agreement nearly 10 years after the original print; O'Hara, 1999), as well as several compilations of punk narratives and interviews (Kuhn, 2010; Peterson, 2009; Sabin, 1999; Sprouse, 1990) detailed the experiences of punks. Lastly, there have been several recent doctoral dissertations written on the topic of punk (Anderson, 2012; England, 2013; Henderson, 2003; Mageary, 2012).

Since punk related scholarship is scattered along a variety of disciplines, with no significant offerings originating from education (specifically curriculum studies), for the purposes of this research, it is most fitting to focus on written works that explore the punk do-it-yourself (DIY) ethic as a potential site of learning. The following section details the importance of the DIY ethic as a primary educational tenet of punk, as well as the ways specific scholarship (which originates outside of education or curriculum studies) connects aspects of punk to what could be interpreted as educative. Although they are broken into segments here in order to discern the nuanced differences, it is important to note that these elements are also inherently entwined and often interdependent on one another.

DIY (Do-It-Yourself) Ethic

> *Stripped to its most basic and empowering elements, punk is the willingness of human beings to challenge their world and themselves, to stand with underdogs and misfits while exploding boundaries, seeking truth relentlessly, and mobilizing grassroots DIY creativity. In the end, punk calls us to stretch beyond the tricks and traps of the world towards a universe of possibilities . . . towards life at its fullest.*
> —Biel, 2012, p. 183

In his detailed account of punk's involvement in political and social issues, *The Philosophy of Punk*, O'Hara discusses the ways in which punk evolved into a DIY philosophy, in addition to a music scene:

> Punk is a formidable voice of opposition. We have created our own music, our own lifestyle, our own community, and our own culture . . . We are building a movement based on love, taking actions in hope that someday peace

may finally be achieved. We may stumble in our efforts, but we still struggle to carry on. Freedom is something we can create every day; it is up to all of us to make it happen. (O'Hara, 1999, p. 25)

Mageary (2012), in his qualitative study on identity construction within punk, further describes DIY as an,

> Ethical and practical stance [that] now pervades punk culture, from booking shows to writing and recording music to the production of clothing, 'zines, and other cultural artifacts. It is such an integral element of punk that many participants cannot separate the two. (Mageary, 2012, p. 63)

Mageary also details how hardcore communities grew into sites of activism by acting as loosely organized social movements based on "DIY ethics and rebellious political and social commentaries," which was an important "shift made by some punks from mere reactionary moving away from the dominant discourse to a more proactive moving toward a new understanding of self, society and punk" (p. 71).

The shift of focus from rebelling against authority to the work of creating (or reconstructing) a world that was more just, allowed for hardcore punk (particularly between the years of 1986 to 1998) to increasingly act as a site of DIY learning. Peterson (2009), in his acclaimed work *Burning Fight: The Nineties Revolution in Ethics, Politics, Spirit, and Sound,* describes the marking of an era when hardcore punks "came to have extremely radical views on topics like animal rights, gender, DIY, race, sprituality. [T]hese ideas were around in the eighties, but many people became even more focused on them in the nineties" (p. 19).

Peterson, an academic as well as a punk insider, was heavily influenced by his own experience in 1990s hardcore where "the individual had the power to take an active role in the scene and claim it as their own" (p. 2). As an entry point into punk's potential connection to DIY learning, I continue to look to Peterson and his published compilation of punk narratives discussing the importance of the DIY concept that "went beyond the boundaries of the scene and became a general philosophy of taking personal ideas, beliefs, and ultimately your life into your own hands" (Peterson, 2009, p. 27).

> Hardcore isn't an aesthetic, its an independent space for kids to develop their own culture.... Hardcore is made up of spaces that kids control and those are outside of the grip of corporations—and I'd like to think, also outside the grip of religious institutions, fascists, etc. (Dingledine, as cited in Peterson, 2009, p. 31)

> The Hardcore scene wasn't just passive consumers—it was kids putting on shows, making 'zines, creating music and artwork. (Beibin, as cited in Peterson, 2009, p. 29)

> Hardcore is all about "doing it yourself." It is at the core of the heart of it all—taking things into your hands, going outside the system, creating something that you believe in with what you have available to you, taking control back into your own hands, expressing yourself honestly and passionately. (Boarts-Larson, as cited in Peterson, 2009, p. 33)

> You have a scene of all these kids figuring out how their lives are impacted by "the man" and how they can, in turn, make some positive changes to neutralize these pressures. It was insane how many kids were voicing their opinions. It created an alternative media that was easy to understand, gave resources to things like how to become vegan, how to scam corporations, and simple "you are not alone" topics...we consumed our time with with these social issues. We spent endless hours molding our daily lives, our social time and our money around a lifestyle fueled by making a difference. (Niemet, as cited in Peterson, 2009, p. 29)

Biel (2012) authored a poignant and contemporary work on DIY punk creation, *Beyond the Music: How Punks Are Saving the World with DIY Ethics, Skills, & Values*, where he collected nearly 40 interviews of adults who identified as being connected to their punk community, as well as inspired by the DIY ethos to fuel productive lives. According to Biel, within his interviews lived a "common thread [of] people talking about obtaining the confidence needed to start what would be a risky or unthinkable venture because of their background in punk and the DIY ethos" (Biel, 2012, p. 108). One of the more poignant interviews was with a punk participant who later became a psychologist, who when asked about the role DIY punk played in his life, reported:

> I got a lot of confidence from punk, embraced the courage it takes to do something you care about, and projects like my 'zine were great learning that you can make something cool happen.... To me, punk at the core represents "another way of doing things than you have been taught," and at least in spirit honors genuine expression at a soul level, and is about balancing the tension of being an individual while also engaging in a community. (Meek, as cited in Biel, 2012, p. 43)

Additional interviews discuss how the "liberating quality" of DIY punk allows for participants to feel as if "you can do anything you want to" (p. 20), in that it provides for the confidence to pursue lifelong dreams (p. 119). Although the interviews do not reference education theory or curriculum directly, Biel's collection is one of few published works that isolates the DIY punk ethos and honors it through rich description of its societal contributions through individual stories.

Although present in all aspects of punk, DIY learning largely manifests in two areas: the punk music scene (as described through shows and lyrics) and punk 'zines. Of primary importance to the historical construction of punk is, of course, the music. As it seems fitting to discuss this founding element first, the following section provides an overview of scholarship that will offer a glimpse into the ways punk shows and music lyrics may act as a site of learning.

Punk Music Scene: Punk Shows and Lyrics

> *Punk has historically been primarily an embodied experience in which attendance at, and participation in, live performance was integral to punk identity formation.*
> —Mageary, 2012, p. 82

While nearly every formal or informal written analysis of punk will address the centrality of the music, there are a select handful of academic works that specifically discuss the importance of the punk music scene to those engaged in punk that are worth mentioning in a conversation addressing the notion of educative spaces. To further delineate the context of this proposed site of learning, I offer the definition of the music scene as put forth by Peterson and Bennett (2004): "The context in which clusters of producers, musicians and fans collectively share their common musical tastes and collectively distinguish themselves from others" (Peterson & Bennett, 2004, p. 1).

Punk Shows

In terms of documentation dedicated to honoring the punk show experience, the most impactful publications are of the visual kind. Collections of photographs showcase several aspects of punk shows, but also act as an archive of punk history, providing opportunities to see events from the "punk vault" of the 1970s and early 1980s (Ercoli, 2003), the three decades of "radical punk style and aesthetic" in California (Cervenka & Jocoy, 2002), to the hardcore scene of Washington, DC, during the 1990s (Andersen & Jenkins, 2001). Holly George-Warren, in her photo collection *Punk 365*, describes the impact of shows on her engagement with punk:

> The message coming from the stage was DIY: pick up a guitar and play in a band, or go home and write about the show for an underground 'zine. Perhaps "do it yourself" is punk's most enduring message—and the one that changed our culture. In addition to plugging in and grabbing the mic,

we gals increasingly began writing about music and documenting the scene with cameras. (George-Warren, 2007, p. 3)

Playing a supportive role to these artistic publications, there are other more traditional forms of scholarship that discuss the role of shows with punk community. Griffin, in *Gendered Performance and Performing Gender in the DIY Punk and Hardcore Music Scene,* describes the way shows impact gender performance and identity,

> The important role of the "audience" at punk shows must be recognized. The punk scene, and the Hardcore scene in particular, is generally characterized by the involvement of the crowd and that includes the (physical) interaction of the crowd with each other as well as with the bands playing. The vocal and physical interaction blurs the boundaries between those "on stage" and those in the "audience"; an altered power dynamic to that which you may expect at non-DIY shows. (Griffin, 2012, p. 71)

A particularly poignant work detailing the power of the punk show is Hancock and Lorr's *More Than Just a Soundtrack: Toward a Technology of the Collective in Hardcore Punk,* which discusses the interplay between the music and the mosh pit (i.e., the physically aggressive dance-like movements located in punk shows). "For many punks, this intensity forms a feedback loop, between music and participants, which helps inspire both feelings of being alive and connectedness" (Hancock & Lorr, 2012, p. 329). Hancock and Lorr also discuss *spatial role reversals,* as an "often overlooked but extremely important musical practice of punk" (p. 337):

> These spatial role reversals for punks are integral to constituting a sense of community and camaraderie. Because the musicians and fans are intertwined, spatial role reversals change the audience from being passive recipients of music, simply receiving it from the distant musicians, to being at the center of the action, and in turn the band members are allowed to participate in the crowds with the dispositions and appreciations of fans.... When a band plays on the floor as opposed to the stage, the collapsing of space heightens emotions as people feel taken over by the music. The proximity these spatial reversals create allow for the band and the audience to blend into one; here individual identity dissolves into the larger community similar to what is seen in moshing and stage diving. Proximity is not just an issue of nearness or farness; rather it provides a sense of social and musical investment. (Hancock & Lorr, 2012, p. 338)

Additionally, Simon, in *Entering the Pit: Slam-Dancing and Modernity,* discusses the nature of slam dancing at punk shows, otherwise referred to as moshing, which operates as a "ritual activity" and form of "cultural communication that is learned through participation, not through reading about them" (Simon, 1997, p. 163). Further, it was and continues to be "through slam-dancing that (primarily) hardcore fans live out an ideology" (p. 158).

It is during these intense community-building shows that punk participants actively engaged with punk lyrics. As described in previous sections, the punk ideology and philosophy is expressed through these types of engagement. When they are politically charged or meant to inspire certain behavior, they then act as hardcore curricula since they reflect socializing forces that educate (Cortes, 1979, 1981). To illustrate the impact of hardcore lyrics on punk participants, two aspects of punk culture that have been almost exclusively shaped by hardcore lyrics—the punk straight edge subsect and the vegan/vegetarian movement—will be reviewed in the following section.

Punk Lyrics: Straight Edge

> I've got the straight edge.
> I'm a person just like you.
> But I've got better things to do
> Than sit around and smoke dope.
> 'Cause I know I can cope.
> Always gonna keep in touch.
> Never want to use a crutch.
> (MacKaye, 1981)

In 1981, founding hardcore band Minor Threat wrote the song "Straight Edge," which vehemently supported a punk lifestyle that abstained from casual sex, drugs, and alcohol. Based purely on this song and the conviction of Minor Threat's lead singer, Ian MacKaye, the straight edge movement quickly spread from Washington, DC, to Boston and then rapidly moved to the West Coast. Punks that identified with straight edge (sXe) took ownership of a symbol (sometimes displayed as a large black "x" marked on the back of the hand or a set of three Xs on clothing/tattoos) that was originally used to identify underage people as being too young to drink in bars (Hanefler, 2004, p. 415). Straight edge punk communities and straight edge bands such as Unity, Uniform Choice, In My Eyes, Project X, and 7 Seconds sprung up during the 1980s and 1990s, all with lyrics that asked straight edge participants to not only understand, but also to be able to articulate and teach the dangers of drug and alcohol addiction.

> Yeah, you do drugs, you know I don't
> Yet it's a trend just 'cos I don't.
> Leave me be, can't you see,
> I hate the way it fuckin' smells

> I hate the way it makes me feel
> Thumbs down to all those drugs you need.
> 7 Seconds
> (Seconds, 1984)

> We were best friends way back when
> Man, times were so much different then
> Smoke a joint after school
> We thought it was so fucking cool
> Go to parties, get stinkin' drunk
> Then I got sick of all that junk
> I wised up and I went straight
> But now me and you just can't relate
> We used to be such good friends
> But now I guess this is where it ends
> So take your pipe and you're fucking keg too
> You say I've changed
> I guess I have
> But for the better
> Where it ends!
> (Porcelly, 1987)

Although there are several works that detail the sXe movement within punk, namely Wood's (2006) *Straightedge Youth: Complexity and Contradictions of a Subculture* and Lahickey's (1997) *All Ages: Reflections on Straight Edge*, sociology scholar Ross Haenfler is considered to be an academic authority on the community with his published works *Rethinking Subcultural Resistance: Core Values of the Straight Edge Movement* (2004) and *Straight Edge: Clean Living Youth, Hardcore punk, and Social Change* (2006). In both of the preceding texts, Haenfler, describes the sXe culture and ideology in several U.S. cities, with a focus on the Denver sXe scene of which he was a member.

Haenfler (2004) discusses the ways in which sXe punks use lyrics as a form of curriculum that inspires self-education in regard to the biological impacts of marijuana, alcohol, and other drugs, the addictive nature of cigarettes, the capitalistic foundation of legal drugs, and the impact of the United States drug economy on Latin American countries (pp. 415–417). In sXe communities, instead of engaging in more individual political protest (i.e., picketing, civil disobedience, petitioning), they act with collective ideological resistance (Haenfler, 2004, p. 418). For instance, rather than challenge tobacco, beer, or beef companies directly, "an sXer refuses their products and might boycott Kraft (parent company of cigarette manufacturer Phillip Morris), adopt a vegetarian lifestyle, or wear a shirt to school reading, 'It's OK not to drink. Straight Edge' or 'Go Vegan'" (Haenfler, 2006, p. 56).

If drinking's what it take to be accepted
I'd rather stay aware and be rejected
I know what it takes to keep my head on straight
Putting shit in my mind and body is not the way
I don't need the drugs, I don't need a crutch
My mind is all I'll ever need to stay in touch
You can laugh but you'll get yours
Reason an excuse for your pressure
Finally, you understand
Drinking doesn't make you a man
Not me, I know what's smart
In touch, I'll always be alert
(Dubar, 1986)

Although the national sXe movement significantly diminished in 1999, Gabriel Kuhn's (2010) *Sober Living for the Revolution: Hardcore Punk, Straight Edge and Radical Politics*, a collection of interviews with several activists and communities of sXe feminists, artists, and musicians that continue to nurture a drug-free lifestyle, acted as part of the resurgence in sXe punk scholarship (Barrett, 2013; Rohrer, 2014).

> The revolutionary call of straight edge, then, as of punk, is that of a place to start, not an ending in itself. Its promise and possibility is to make us strong to go out into other communities, able to listen, learn, and grow, even as we try to bring broader social change. (Kuhn, 2010, p. 298)

Punk Lyrics: Veganism/Vegetarianism

But you cannot deny that meat is still murder.
Dairy is still rape.
I have recognized one form of oppression.
Now I recognize the rest.
And life's too short to make another's shorter.
(Propaghandi, 1996)

As part of the progressive hardcore punk movement of the 1990s, bands such as Propaghandi, Good Clean Fun, Earth Crisis, and The Locust were performing songs consisting of lyrics focused on animal rights, vegan and vegetarian diets, and the dangers of processed food (Haenfler, 2006; Kuhn, 2010; Wood, 2006)). One of the earliest works analyzing the impact of hardcore lyrics is McDonald's (1987) *Suicidal Rage: An Analysis of Hardcore Punk Lyrics*, which was advanced by the recent scholarship of Cherry (2006) and Clark (2004, 2013) that detail the connections between animal rights activism and punk community norms and values:

> In the punk underground, food serves to elaborate and structure ideologies about how the world works. Through a complex system of rules, suggestions, and arguments, punk cuisine spelled out on a plate its ideologies. (Clark, 2004, p. 20)

Interviews with punk musicians offer insight not otherwise seen in academic scholarship, including, perhaps with great specificity, the educative impact lyrics has on activism. In a 2009 interview with the People for the Ethical Treatment of Animals (PETA), Justin Pearson, lead singer of The Locust, shared that becoming vegan was directly related to his engagement with the punk community:

> I think what turned me on to vegetarian politics were aspects of the punk community. The main thing was a band called Downcast, as well as No Answers fanzine. Originally, I wasn't concerned with health issues and eating well. But as I was turned on to—and became educated about—the politics of vegetarian eating, I became more and more upset at the meat industry and factory farming, as well as the corporations that test products on animals and the universities that use animals for experiments. (PETA, 2009)

Having been exposed to animal rights punk curriculum through hardcore lyrics that they listened to as younger participants in a punk community, members of The Locust use their own lyrics to instruct:

> Massive production for human consumption.
> pesticidal waste, what once was fertile earth.
> defiled farmland won't sustain life.
> what can you do to end the hunger?
> it's no surprise that many will die with the coming shortage of food.
> when there is no grain to feed the butchered cows,
> when there is no grain to feed yourselves,
> then you will see that money can't be eaten
> (Pearson, 2004)

Youth of Today, one of the most well-known hardcore bands who were committed to animal rights, discusses their process to include their beliefs in their lyric creation:

> Me and Ray were both vegetarians, so we thought it was an important thing. Ray, he wanted to write a song about vegetarianism, and…we were even, like…Are people gonna take to this, or are they gonna take it, like, completely strange? And then, it was another idea whole time had come…I think it's a testament to the power of music. Music has such a power to change and influence people's lives. It's amazing. (Porcelly, as cited in Wood, 2006, p. 39)

> Meat eating, flesh eating, think about it
> so callous to this crime we commit
> always stuffing our face with no sympathy
> what a selfish, hardened society so
> No. More. (Cappo, 1988)

Punk lyrics, as conveyed through the insider and academic scholarship outlined above, acted as a form of curriculum within a larger community site of learning. Moving forward to explore a more tangible DIY creation of the punk 'zine, which in the context of DIY punk culture is the focus of considerable scholarship, is outlined in the following section.

Punk 'Zines

> *The DIY ethic of punk culture, the bucking of mainstream acceptance, and the newly minted pejorative "selling out" all gave credence to 'zines as the official voice of punk culture—or at least as official as it was going to get.*
> —Moore, 2010, p. 246

> *Eventually I came across an issue of Maximum Rocknroll and something changed inside of me.*
> —Peterson, 2009, p. 2

Punk 'zines (first taken from the word fanzine, but later changed to punkzine or 'zine), are community produced and published magazines devoted to punk culture, music, bands, or the DIY punk ethic (Laing, 1978; Mageary, 2012; Moore and Roberts, 2009). Britain's *NME (New Musical Express)*, created in 1952, may be one of the longest running magazines to cover music news; although *NME* and the magazine *Melody Maker* were not self-published fanzines, they were closely connected with the early punk movement in England and the United States. *NME* and *Melody Maker* operated as inspiration for the DIY mid-1970s creations of punk 'zines in Britain (e.g., *Sniffin' Glue*) and several U.S. cities.

One of the earliest U.S. based punk 'zines was the New York magazine *Punk*. It was first published in 1976 and was largely created to promote the early New York underground music scene. In order to foster a dynamic punk scene in the United States, *Punk* drew attention to bands such as the Ramones and the New York Dolls by labeling them as punk. *Flipside* (1977–2000) was one of the longest running punk 'zines and chronicled the Los Angeles punk scene; it now operates as *Razorcake* (when it was ressurected by the former managing editor in 2001). In 1983, Aaron Elliot founded the 'zine *Cometbus*; many argue it is the longest running punk 'zine. It recently celebrated its 25th anniversary and chronicles the California Bay area punk scene. *Cometbus* is distinctly DIY as it is one of the few 'zines primarily using handwritten text (examples of *Cometbus* writing were used in punk band liner notes in the 1990s). During the early-1980s through the early-1990s hardcore punk scene, 'zines continued to promote punk ethics and politics though national 'zines such the anarchist *Profane Existence* and the hardcore specific 'zine *HeartattaCk* (the "h" and the "c" are capitalized for the abbreviation of "hardcore"). These two publications were among the most important fanzines in the 1990s.

Maximum Rocknroll, a 'zine known for its political columns and reader submissions, further contributed to a larger community-wide ideological conversation:

> The only thing that threatens a society based on dividing and conquering—pitting sex against sex, race against race, subculture against subculture—is unity. If the system stresses anti- intellectualism, then we must become intellectuals. If it stresses isolation and ignorance of each other, then we must learn to trust. If it stresses individualism, we must collect ourselves. If it stresses blind respect for authority, we must only give respect to those who earn it. If punk is to be a threat, different from society, then any so-called punk who flirts with racism and sexism, proudly displays ignorance, resorts to physical violence and is afraid of knowledge or political action, is not a threat at all, but has gone over to the enemy. (*Maximum Rocknroll*, as cited in Moore & Roberts, 2009)

Punk Planet, one of the largest and longest running U.S. based 'zines (published from 1994–2007) was substantially the most comprehensive punk 'zine focusing on music reviews. Additionally, it included overt political articles detailing columnists' reflections on labor relations, race issues, gender formation, sexual orientation, and anticorporate media. *Punk Planet* nurtured a formidable attempt at gathering punk community across the United States. With its fiction section (available for submission by punk authors) and its online presence, *Punk Planet* embraced punk ideals of activism and community with its readers

In addition to these national titles, most local scenes have informal self-published 'zines with opinion columns, band interviews with local or touring bands, and music reviews. Punk 'zines quickly became the primary mode of communication on the national and local levels of the punk movement. The punk 'zine is very accessible by nature. The participation in 'zines ranged from publishing to reviewing to reading. By creating or contributing to a 'zine, a punk could simultaneously be in a band, be a music journalist, and a music critic. In addition to living in the collective community mind, 'zines have been the focus of academic research, specifically in reference to advancing the practice of DIY publishing as an empowering autobiographical practice (Stockburger, 2011) and as a curriculum tool for the English classroom (Buchanan & Fink, 2012; Wan, 1999).

Additionally, zines were primary topics in scholarship concerned with feminism and gender identity construction, and performance (Schilt & Zobl, 2008; Zobl 2001, 2004a, 2009). According to Comstock (2001), in "Grrrl Zine Networks: Re-Composing Spaces of Authority, Gender, and Culture," by "seizing the production and distribution practices of countercultural publishing and strategically mixing the popular and political, grrrl 'zinesters point to the possibility of social change within commercial, academic, and mainstream feminist contexts" (Comstock, 2001, p. 404). Kylie Lewis, creator of the 'zine *Personality Liberation Front*, discussed the intention for her written work:

> It is my strong belief that DIY 'zine projects affirm both a sense of self and a sense of community. I really think they are such an excellent medium for challenging mainstream norms and expressing radical opinions... when we start to become aware that what we say and do matters, and that we can change ourselves and others via our personal/political activities. (Lewis, as cited in Schilt & Zobl, 2008, p. 181)

What may lend itself to viewing 'zines as a component of a site of learning (i.e., 'zines could be seen as a more knowledgable other [MKO]) for a community of committed and invested individuals, is Moore and Roberts' (2009) assertion in *Do-it-Yourself Mobilization: Punk and Social Movements*, that 'zines contribute to punk's "mobilization" as a communal social movement (p. 275). Additionally, Zobl (2001, 2004a, 2004d) and Moore (2007) describe hardcore punk 'zines as powerful tools that promote norms and community values, specifically reflecting the DIY aesthetic of punk by created a thriving underground press that brings punk participants together:

> Nationally circulated 'zines such as *Maximum Rocknroll* and *Flipside* regularly solicited "scene reports" from everywhere, from midsized California suburbs to Eastern European nations, thus not only keeping readers abreast of events in their hometown but also reminding them that they were part of a larger imagined community. (Moore, 2007, p. 453)

Contextual evidence of Moore's descriptions exist as, even though *Razorcake* has primarily interviewed bands during its 13-year history, many issues will have at least one interview with a popular academic icon chosen by the editors. For example, *Razorcake* issue #40 (2007) contains an interview with renowned historian Howard Zinn, while issue #57 (2010) hosts an interview with political activist Noam Chomsky. Carswell, cofounder of *Razorcake*, builds on the importance of interviews as an educative force:

Music is, of course, always first for *Razorcake*, but ideology runs a very close second. If you just read the interviews of the bands, a lot of time it is because the music is good. But their music is good because they're part of a community that has a certain ideology and they learn the music from that community and then they express or build on or engage with that ideology in the interviews. So you'll notice, if you read interviews, they are largely not about music, instead, they are more about lifestyles, building a culture—and by culture, I mean kind of the stories we tell ourselves about ourselves. What stories do we want to use to define us? That's what these interviews are. (Personal communication, May 12, 2010)

Interviews were the main source of disseminating content knowledge within *Razorcake*, and could then be considered implicit or outside curriculum (Eisner, 1994; Schubert, 1981, 2010) as there is little within the interview texts that explicitly tell participant learners to behave, look, or demonstrate knowledge in any certain way; however, since the interviewer and the interviewee are in conversation (perhaps Pinar [2008] would describe it as a "complicated conversation") about punk identity, culture, and ideology, readers were then allowed to make inferences about what is important to know, and then further use the knowledge to guide the norms of their engagement.

> Speaking from my experience, I was a naïve little girl before and I'd never thought 'zines have helped me changed my perceptions towards a number of things that I could hardly find in the mainstream media. Like a few years ago, for the first time I learned about the notorious McDonalds and bloodsucking Nike in a local punk 'zine, or the mass killing in Acheh (Indonesia) and Tibet. Believe it or not, I was inspired to pick up guitar and form my own punk band after reading a Riot Grrrl 'zine. (Zobl, 2001)

In the previous sections, I offer scholarship and community-based evidence that focuses on aspects of the punk community, culture, and values which may be inferred to act as either curriculum or a site of learning, however, there is no more important component of punk culture than that which calls participants to direct action based on their newfound knowledge. The section that follows discusses the ways in which punk curriculum informed action, by individuals or communities, as evidenced by creation of or involvement in activist organizations.

Punk-Based Activist Organizations

> *We try to live this idea, to preach our gospel—as it were—with our actions, and not with our self-righteous rhetoric.*
> —Andersen, as cited in Kuhn, 2010, p. 298

Caumont (2005) describes punk as a "culture of conflict" where it can be simultaneously "conformist and non-conformist; focused and directionless; caring and oblivious; intelligent and idiotic; anarchic and structured–there are many rules to being a punk in that there are specific opinions and beliefs that punks are obligated and pressured to share" (para. 3). Caumont's criticism may well be accurate of the movement in general terms, yet for many punks, listening to punk music and internalizing the lyrics also meant doing more then passively identifying as punk, it meant becoming a social justice advocate and activist on behalf of causes that were aligned with the punk philosophy (see O'Hara, 1999). This activism often manifested into the creation of organizational efforts. Given the inconsistent smattering of punk scholarship amongst disciplines, the academic works discussing the spectrum of punk political activism is surprisingly deep; however, for the purpose of this section, I will focus on three of the most prolific DIY organizational commitments (formal and informal) of punk action: CrimethInc. Ex-Workers Collective, Riot Grrrl!, and Food Not Bombs (FNB).

CrimethInc. Ex-Workers Collective

> *I wrote short stories and made 'zines with other punks and artists. One day I woke up wondering how the punk rock anti-corporate scene could change anything if all we did was party. How was this any different from the mainstream? That was when I first encountered anarchism through a guerrilla text producer called CrimethInc.*
>
> —Jeppesen, 2011, p. 24

Created in the mid to late-1990s, (the exact year is unknown), CrimethInc. Ex-Workers Collective (CWC) was birthed from social justice activism within the Northwest (particularly the cities of Seattle, Washington, and Portland, Oregon) and the Southeast (Atlanta, Georgia) punk communities, with a focus on fighting capitalism and corporate interests on a local level. During this particular era of punk activism (1995–2005), regional anticorporate rallies and protests were becoming more and more commonplace; *Adbusters* (an anticonsumerism magazine created in 1989), Naomi Klein's (2000) anticorporate branding book *No Logo*, and published works and films criticizing corporate food giants (Bove & Dufour, 2001; Schlosser, 2001; Spurlock, 2004) propelled the resistance to capitalistic control to a national level.

On November 30, 1999, protests in the Northwest United States made international news when:

> a radical coalition of students, youth, feminists, environmental, labor, anarchist, queer, and human rights activists converged on Seattle. The target:

the system of global capitalism. In blocking the meetings of the World Trade Organization, a movement was ignited. (Shepard & Hayduck, 2002, p. 1)

When the protest was over a few days later, more than 500 people had been arrested and the damage to commercial buildings (many corporate storefronts, such as Starbucks and The Gap, had been physically targeted) in Seattle was estimated at over $20 million.

Although several articles reference CrimethInc. as part of punk activism (Portwood-Stacer 2012; Schill, 2012; Thompson 2004), the primary academic work discussing CrimethInc. as an important collective is Jeppesen's (2011) *The DIY Post-Punk Post-Situationist Politics of CrimethInc*. Jeppesen describes CrimethInc. as a predominantly

> White, middle-class, post-punk, post-situationist group of loosely affiliated cells that produce cultural texts and events (p. 26) [that is] wary of the way punk music has been co-opted by corporations...they reject the mainstreaming of punk but maintain the DIY ethic of self-determination. (Jeppesen, 2011, p. 29)

CrimethInc. Ex-Workers Collective (CWC) operates as an organization with agents and cells within the United States, Canada, and Europe with the intention of liberating people from the corporate created culture through the production of DIY texts that detail ways in which punks (or other like-minded anarchists) can subvert the dominant capitalist economic system. Unlike other punk activist organizations, CrimethInc. focused on nurturing rebellion through individual actions that are often illegal and that thwart adherence to consumerism and government authority. CrimethInc. describes itself as

> the transgression without which freedom and self-determination are impossible—it is the skeleton key that unlocks the prisons of our age. CrimethInc. is the black market where we trade in this precious contraband. Here, the secret worlds of shoplifters, rioters, dropouts, deserters, adulterers, vandals, daydreamers—that is to say, of all of us, in those moments when, wanting more, we indulge in little revolts—converge to form gateways to new worlds where theft, cheating, warfare, boredom, and so on are simply obsolete. (CrimethInc, 2013)

As its primary way of reaching its current and prospective members, CrimethInc. publishes written texts that educate members of the collective on political, economic, and environmental issues, as well as clearly instructs them (often with step-by-step diagrams) on the best ways to dumpster dive for food or shoplift without being arrested:

CrimethInc. publishes broadsheets such as *Hunter/Gatherer, Harbinger* and *A Civilian's Guide to Direct Action*, and 'zines such as the manifesto *Fighting for our Lives*, graffiti how-to "The Walls are Alive," and do-it-yourself or DIY guides I and II, which include instructions for everything from punk stitching with dental floss to smashing capitalism. CrimethInc. also produces activist videos such as *PickAxe*, an anti-logging documentary, and the anti-free-trade documentary, *Breaking the Spell: Eugene, Anarchists and the WTO*... More recently they have begun to publish a biannual magazine called *Rolling Thunder*, an anarchist journal of dangerous living. (Jeppesen, 2011, p. 26)

The CrimethInc. written works are rarely attributed to specific members or "agents," rather CrimethInc. is the author and also often the publisher. Located in Salem, Oregon, CrimethInc. Far East is the current operating headquarters for the collective and they continue to print and distribute their most sought after guides (also available for free on their website as downloads): "A Civilian's Guide to Direct Action" (a step-by-step guide for protesting and organizing) and "The Walls Are Alive: A How-To Graffiti Guide For Those Who Scheme and Those Who Dream" (a guide for those who want to create street art via posters or graffiti with details on how to avoid getting caught by the police).

Riot Grrrl! (1992–1996)

Hardcore opened up doors for women in ways the first and second waves of punk struggled to, as it was in the third wave of punk that women-fronted bands became more common, as well as a generalized acknowledgement and fight against sexism (Peterson, 2009; Willis, 1993). The DIY ethic specifically impacted women punks in their own evolution as learners and participants. The creation and evolution of Riot Grrrl! is well covered in academic texts and books before 2000 (see Rosenberg & Garafola, 1998; Scott-Dixon, 1999; Wald & Gottlieb, 1993) and there are recent works that offer current perspectives on the feminist punk informal organization (Downes, 2012; Marcus, 2010; Nguyen, 2012; Strong, 2011; Zobl, 2004a). Additionally, several dissertations have explored Riot Grrrl! (D'Angelica 2009; Garrett 2011), but the most detailed and authentic representation of this era is chronicled by punk 'zines (e.g., *Jigsaw, Girl Germs, Bikini Kill*).

According to Monem (2007), LeBlanc (1999), and Schilt and Zobl (2008), the feminist punk subgenre Riot Grrrl! was a localized third-wave feminist network originating from the male-dominated punk rock scene. In Zobl's (2004c) *Revolution Grrrl and Lady Style, Now!*, Riot Grrrl is described as a movement with "no officially structured organization; there were no leaders, membership rules, or regulations. Anyone who identified with feminism, punk, queerness, and Riot Grrrl ideals could participate" (Zobl, 2004c, p. 447). In her work *Riot Grrrl, Race, and Revival*, Nguyen (2012) reviews the academic chronicle of Riot Grrrl! as well as an updated analysis of the movement.

> [A] new strain of punk feminism, weary of both the soul-crushing criterion of commodity culture and the masculine bravado of punk subculture distancing girls from knowing themselves and one another, posed the solution through the promise of do-it-yourself—that is, make music, make art, make the world, make yourself. Girls pushed their way to the front and onto the stage with guitars in hand; girls sent concealed dollar bills in exchange for each other's passionate manifestos passing as cut-and-pasted zines; girls traded mixed tapes of favorite bands, and each song, and every page, was a revelation. Doing it yourself made it possible to know yourself as a revolutionary act. (Nguyen, 2012, p. 175)

Riot Grrrls created network chapters across the United States connecting young women with punk music, a thriving 'zine scene, political action, and feminist ideologies. Marcus (2010), in Chapter 6 of her celebrated book *Girls to the Front: The True Story of the Riot Grrrl Revolution*, details how the Riot Grrrl elder community (chapter leaders, local activists whom Vygotsky might consider MKOs) also taught feminist literacy skills, via meetings and conventions; these social interactions included social networking to put on Riot Grrrl shows, 'zine making, and activism strategies:

> The first national Riot Grrrl convention took place the final weekend of July [1992]. Over a hundred girls attended, possibly more like two hundred-there was no formal sign-in where they might have been counted, just a little tri-folded piece of paper with a map of the DuPont Circle area...some of the girls were from DC, but many more were girls like Christina Woolner, who took a Peter Pan bus down from New York...Saturday was packed with discussions and workshops at the Peace Center. (These sessions were girls only; meanwhile, a nascent Positive Force Men's group, helmed by Mark Andersen, facilitates a concurrent mini-convention for guys to talk about sexism, homophobia, rape, male sexuality, and *Thelma and Louise*.) An hour-long discussion about sexuality kicked things off for the girls at 10:30. Then, after a 10-minute break, the group reconvened for an emotional session bluntly titled "Rape." (Marcus, 2010, pp. 162–165)

In addition to the chapter meetings and conventions, Riot Grrl publications were also a site of DIY learning. According to Marcus (2010), nearly 40,000 Riot Grrrl 'zines were self-published during the peak of the movement (p. 296); 'zines played a crucial role in bringing together girls and women across the country who shared an interest in creating "punk rock feminism" because the written work of 'zines were considered a "written record of their life" (Zobl, 2004d, p. 175).

For many Riot Grrrls, feminist punk 'zines prompted their first thoughts on gender issues. In an interview with 'zine creator Kylie Lewis (2004), she describes how Riot Grrrl aided in her feminism education.

> My first exposure to zines was through an independent toy-comic-DIY-'zine store (Silver Rocket) in my hometown Brisbane when I was 16, and I picked up a copy of *Grot Grrrl*, a 'zine from Melbourne, Australia, which really inspired me. It had a really pro-grrrl attitude, with an emphasis on building a network of grrrl bands, supporting wimmin in DIY art/culture/punk, supporting wimmin in prison and other political struggles (Lewis, as cited in Zobl, 2004b).

In her epilogue, Marcus (2010) describes the last years of Riot Grrrl. It is generally thought that Riot Grrl ended sometime in 1996 when chapter meetings stopped occurring and the movement in general seemed to dissipate; popular Riot Grrrl bands broke-up and the girls grew older and into their more mature lives:

> People grew out of Riot Grrrl, but that doesn't diminish the movement's value... Riot Grrrl, by encouraging girls to turn their anger outward, taught a crucial lesson. Always ask: Is there something wrong, not with me, but with the world at large? It also forced us to confront a second question: Once we've found our rage, where do we go from there? (p. 329)

Food Not Bombs (1980–Present)

> *Above all, the Food Not Bombs experience is an opportunity for self-empowerment.*
> —McHenry, 2013, p. 33

In his preface to the first Food Not Bombs handbook, *Food Not Bombs* (Butler & McHenry, 2000), Howard Zinn argues:

> The message of Food Not Bombs is simple and powerful: no one should be without food in a world so richly provided with land, sun, and human ingenuity. No consideration of money, no demand for profit, should stand in the way of any hungry or malnourished child or any adult in need. Here are people who will not be bamboozled by "the laws of the market" that say only people who can afford to buy something can have it. (Butler & McHenry, 2000, p. xi)

Food Not Bombs (FNB), as a nearly four-decade-old activist organization, collects surplus food from bakeries, grocers, and food banks to disseminate publicly to anyone in need (usually those who are homeless), is discussed briefly in several articles, books, and cookbooks (Flores, 2006; Forson & Counihan, 2013; Moskowitz, 2005; Pfeiffer, 2006); however, in relation to punk and anarchist communities, there are a few autobiographical sources (CrimethInc., 2001; Himelstein, 1998; Ott, 2000) and even fewer academic sources that are comprehensive in their analysis (Heynen, 2010; Clark, 2004). For many who seek to understand FNB, the best source is McHenry's (2012) *Hungry for Peace*, which is currently in its third edition and written by an original FNB cofounder.

Although FNB's creative roots are not exclusively punk, it has become an activist site of learning for many regional punk and anarchist-punk communities. Founded in New Mexico in 1980, the food distribution organization was created when cofounder Brian Feigenbaum was arrested at the May 24 Direct Action to Stop Seabrook Nuclear Station in New Hampshire, which "inspired bake sales to raise money for Brian's defense" (McHenry, 2012, p. 153). A year later, FNB started formalizing their bake sales as protests against companies and banks who were supporting nuclear weapon technologies; food was given away during the protests and street theater performances. In its contemporary life, according to Heynen (2009):

> FNB is one of the most rapidly growing direct action social movements working against the politics of [food] containment. Ideologically based in anarchist principles of mutual aid there are now perhaps as many as 400 autonomous FNB chapters sharing food throughout North, Central and South America, Europe, Africa, the Middle East, Asia, and Australia .(p. 1227)

In the 2012 edition of *Hungry for Peace* (originally published in 1992), McHenry details the history of FNB, the commitment to nonviolent direct action and the political statements that are inherent to FNB organizing.

> Food Not Bombs volunteers respond to poverty and lack of self-esteem in at least two ways. First, we provide food in an open, respectful way to whomever wants it without restriction, rich or poor, sober or not. We will not make people jump through any bureaucratic hoops designed to control, humiliate, and often punish people without money. Second, we invite people who receive the food to become involved in participating in the collection, cooking or sharing of the food. (McHenry, 2012, p. 18)

FNB has the following three principles that have been adhered to since they were formally created at the 1992 Food Not Bombs International Gathering in San Francisco.

1. The food is always vegan or vegetarian and free to everyone without restriction, rich or poor, stoned or sober.

2. Food Not Bombs has no formal leaders or headquarters, and every group is autonomous and makes decisions using the consensus process.
3. Food Not Bombs is dedicated to nonviolent direct action and works for nonviolent social change.

FNB is firm about only supplying vegan or vegetarian meals because it is an organizational tenet that "changing to a vegan diet is one effective way to reduce hunger since it is possible to feed many more people on less land and with less water on a plant-based diet than one that relies on meat production" (McHenry, 2012, p. 27). McHenry adds:

> While we encourage awareness of vegan and vegetarian living for political and economic reasons, this policy also has several more immediate and practical benefits. The potential for problems with food spoilage are greatly reduced when dealing strictly with vegetables, fruit and other vegan foods. Our volunteers tend to eat a more healthy diet as they learn more about vegetarianism. Our diet reflects our desire to promote a non-violent future. Teaching people about the health benefits of a vegan and vegetarian diet actually creates a healthy, caring attitude towards ourselves, others, and the planet as a whole. (McHenry, 2012, p. 27)

McHenry provides logistics around collecting food, examples of how to give the food away, as well as detailed chapters on engagement with governmental agencies and the police. Information on how to create a FNB chapter (with models from Boston and San Francisco to Nairobi and Reykjavik) and the importance of meetings run by consensus decision-making are central to the last half of the handbook; at the end of the handbook, vegetarian and vegan recipes (e.g., potato soup, apple crisp and homemade tofu) are provided for those who wish to cook food as a complement to the collected food items. Heynen (2010), in his article "Cooking up Non-Violent Civil-Disobedient Direct Action for the Hungry: 'Food Not Bombs' and the Resurgence of Radical Democracy in the U.S.," discusses the political statement made by FNB by detailing the East Coast FNB chapters' description of their work:

> Our meals are served outdoors. This is for a number of reasons: to show the larger public that hunger is a daily problem that people must deal with, and [in their case] to fulfill the mission of People's Park [Berkeley, California] as a place where people can go to meet the needs of the body. The weekday meals in People's Park where most folks sit in little groups on the grass encourage an open, community spirit. It runs counter to the usual practice of hiding poor people away in church basements while they get a meal. (Gans & Karacas, as cited in Heynen, 2010, p. 1229)

Heynen continues to explain the role FNB plays in social justice activism.

While civil disobedience is not exactly the same as direct action, they are not fully separable. It is within their tactical coming together under an explicit commitment to non-violence that they can be an even more powerful force for social change than either individually. (Heynen, 2010, p. 1235)

FNB's connection to punk is largely known only to insiders and is not overly analyzed in academic discourse, except for a few places when discussing anarchist punks' desire to participate in direct action against the consumerist culture, the food justice movement, and animal rights. According to Clark in his article "The Raw and the Rotten: Punk Cuisine,"

> A variety of activist groups had a symbiotic relationship to punk culture. One of the foremost was Food Not Bombs. Like other anarchist dis-organizations, Food Not Bombs can be set up by anyone—anyone willing to collect, prepare, and distribute free food to the homeless and the hungry. (Clark, 2004, p. 12)

FNB matched punk ideology further on an economic and international level:

> For punks, mainstream food is epitomized by corporate-capitalist "junk food" and the extraordinary geographies that come together in such products. Punks regularly liken mainstream food geographies to colonialism, in their impacts on the Third World: destruction of rainforests (allegedly cleared for beef production), the creation of cash-cropping (to service World Bank debts), and cancer (in the use of banned pesticides on unprotected workers and water supplies). Furthermore, punks allege, rangeland and agribusiness plantations destroy whole ecosystems. (Clark, 2004, p. 3)

Critique of Punk: Race and Whiteness

> *Race, in punk, is like outer space: this distant constellation of "issues" clustered way, way out there.*
> —Mimi Nguyen, 1999

> *The general tendencies of most white punks tend to be to settle for the symbolic, and fail to support the real struggles of people to change the world precisely because they have a choice as opposed to people who have to struggle for their livelihood.*
> —Otto Nomous, 2007

Punk, although lauded in academic texts and insider publications for the prevalence of self-empowerment, community unity, and social justice work, is not without significant critique from both punk community members and scholars. Because this book explores the lived experience of educative punk, the most important critique to discuss here is that of the inherent Whiteness and privilege-denying that lives within the foundation and infrastructure of punk.

To critique punk is to start with the assumption that racism is foundational within the infrastructure of United States cultural institutions and that identifying as punk, in and of itself, does not transcend or explicitly counter the power dynamics within the socially constructed ideas of race and the lived experience of racism. When attempting to understand the evolution of punk's commitment to social justice activism, one important aspect of the historical origins of punk ideology is to remember that it originally revolved entirely around personal and individual economic issues (first wave punk), rather than political or communal aims. These personal issues of White teenage males heavily framed the late-1970s and early-1980s punk movements; so when punks moved into overt political activism in the mid-to late-1980s, the imprint of White male strife framed nearly every aspect.

In consideration of the contemporary core of *punk ethos transmission* (Wood, 2006), we see a mantra of the antiracist, antisexist, anticapitalist activist who conciously rejects the "acting and looking White" because it has been conflated with the "acting and looking wealthy" (Traber, 2001, p. 38). However, by associating Whiteness with everything antipunk, punks allow for an ideology that seemingly offers White punks the choice to opt-out of Whiteness and all of the privileges awarded, yet Whiteness ideology remains deeply embedded. To further illustrate this idea, Nguyen, a self identified Asianqueergirltomboy, remarks:

> To get our official [punk] membership card, we're supposed to give up or put certain parts of ourselves aside—or at least assign them to a secondary rung... Differences are seen as potentially divisive. Some—like race or gender—are seen as more divisive than others.... Of course, this "common culture" is not really that common at all. Whiteness falls into a a "neutral" category, and race is a property that somehow belongs only to "others." So this abstract, conformist citizenship offered by punk to someone like me is a one-handed affair—it all depends on how I want to narrate my raced, sexed, and gendered body into these supposedly democratic communities. If I keep my mouth shut and don't "make an issue" of it, I'm told that I'll get along fine—and never mind the psychic erasures I might have to endure. (Nguyen, 1999)

Nomous (2007) has additional critiques as he challenges the authenticity of punk's commitment to antiracist actions when he accuses punks of not working for the social change relating to issues of covert racism, sexism, living wage, and health care. Nomous asserts that punks "are often more interested in promoting so-called revolutionary organizations than working to provide real alternatives among everyday people...for this reason, [punk] is not very relevant to the actual lives of most oppressed people" (para. 4). Nomous goes on to say punk movements "will not solve racism without the people affected by it. And we certainly won't be seeing any kind of a revolution." (para. 9).

Nguyen further explores punk hypocrisy by calling out the White punks who are confident in their speaking about people of color, while avoiding their own complicity in systems of domination. Nguyen exposes punk privilege by asking punks to reconsider the misguided belief that,

> [Y]ou can extract yourself from the context of social relations and imagine yourself the sole shaper of your fate. It's [this] kind of attitude that puts big obstacles in the way of asking the critical questions about why punk is largely White, heterosexual, and male, and why punk's politics look the way they do. (Nguyen, 1999, p. 9)

In the pursuit of problematizing the contemporary boundaries of punk activism rooted in Whiteness, punk scholars have invited community members to forego what has been described as the "most famous liberal response to the question of race," otherwise knows as the *shrug*. This shrug is further defined as the "color-blind approach that would have us believe 'we're all just human' or, in this case, 'we're all just punk'" and instead promote the punk culture of dissent "to involve some self-reflexive unpacking of privileges/poverties" and their historical and political contexts in order to address punk value hypocrisy (Nguyen, 1999).

As one piece of this unpacking, works detailing the lived experience and oral histories of punks of color (some specifically referencing Vietnamese and Chican@ punk comunities in Los Angeles) have been brought to the forefront of punk scholarship (Alvarado, 2012; Bag, 2011, 2014; Duncombe & Tremblay, 2011). Additionally there has also been a strong formalized movement, Afro-punk, that intentionally challenges the Whiteness of punk (McNeil, 2004; Ramirez-Sanchez, 2008; Thompson, 2010) and privileges the Black punk experience. Afro-punk (2007) exclaims: "Punk Music is Black Music! Afro-punk is a platform for the other Black experience, the one we don't see in our media. DIY (do it yourself) is the foundation."

Collecting Stories

The History and Aims of Phenomenology

> *Perhaps it was as a teacher of English that I came to see stories and the details of people's lives as a way of knowing and understanding.*
> —Seidman, 2006, p. 1

> *An existing individual is constantly in the process of becoming.*
> —Kierkegaard, 1974, p. 79

Like Seidman, I have always been drawn to the ways people describe moments in their lives; perhaps it was nurtured by my own practice as an English teacher, where I yearned to have students enjoy the story so that they could see their own life as a work of art. With this attachment to story in mind, I found phenomenological interviewing as the means which best matched my work as its approach asks scholars to consider "what is the meaning, structure, and essence of the lived experience of a phenomenon for this person or group of people" (Patton, 2002, p. 104).

Phenomenology isolates and honors the typical in everyday life and offers a research methodology and framework to better understand how people experience the things of life that are often taken for granted (Crotty, 2004). The origins of phenemonology are rooted in 19th century German philosophy, specifically through the work of Edmund Husserl (1859–1938) and, his protégé, Martin Heidegger (1889–1976). For Husserl, phenomenology involved the detailed examination of the human experience. Husserl argued that philosophers should "go back to the things themselves"; the things being what he considered the objective reality experienced by people. In other words, Husserl was particularly interested in understanding how a person might become conscious of their own experience, assuming that the experience lived outside of a context or interpretation could be approached in its own right. Husserl and his peers were foundational thinkers of what has been referred to as transcendental phenomenology.

As phenomenological methodology progressed, Husserl's student, Martin Heidegger advanced the ways in which the experience could be conceived and articulated. In *Being and Time*, Heidegger (1927/1962) took on an etymological definition of phenomenology in that "the word [phenomenology] is made up of two parts, derived from the Greek *phenomenon* and *logos*. Phenomenon can be translated as 'show' or 'appear'" (Smith, Flowers, & Larkin, 2009, pp. 483–485). According to Heidegger, the essence of the experience, or the phenomena, "appears" through the facilitation and interpretation of the researcher. Heidegger shifted phenomonology toward a perspective that honored the experience as subjective by nature, and asserted that it could best be understood through interpretation rather that objective awareness. Heidegger was more concerned with the "ontological question of existence itself, and with the practical activities and relationships which we are caught up in, and through which the world appears to us, and is made meaningful" (pp. 321–323).

In this vein, Heidegger and others constructed what has become known as hermeneutic phenomenology. Although there are several additional philosophers (many aligned with existentialism) who advanced both Husserl's and Heidegger's concepts, for the purpose of this book, I reference contemporary phenomenologists Max van Manen and Clark Moustakas whose works evolved from Heidegger's philosophy of phenomenology.

Punk Phenomenology

Phenomenology is a unique and appropriate method to research topics in education since, as articulated by Seidman, "educational issues are abstractions based on the concrete experience of people" (Seidman, 2006, p. 7), which matches the phenomenologist's focus on "descriptions of what people experience and how it is that they experience what they experience" (Patton, 2006, p. 107). In addition to this method acting in the service of education research, interview-based methodology is also a fitting and comfortable method of inquiry already in use within the punk community. According to Carswell (personal communication, 2011), cofounder of the punk 'zine *Razorcake*, interviews provide context to culture and experience, and are instrumental in articulating the positionality of the punks, their ideology, and the ways in which they see the world. Carswell states interviews are "rarely about the music," but rather, they educate about the complexities of being a driving force in the punk community. In addition, interviews maintain the intimacy within the punk community—learners feel close and connected to bands when they are sharing their stories.

In essence, punk 'zines already utilize phenomenological aspects within their publications; this allows my work to sit comfortably within current punk community communication practices. Based on these affirmations, I chose to utilize Seidman's in-depth, phenomenologically based interviewing, which combines life-history interviewing and focused, in-depth interviewing informed by assumptions drawn from phenomenology (Seidman, 2006, p. 15).

Phenomenological In-Depth Interviewing

In-depth, phenomenologically-based interviewing primarily uses open-ended questions that build upon and explore experience. Seidman's (2006) in-depth interview protocol consists of a three interview series: Interview 1, focused life history; Interview 2, the details of experience; and Interview 3, reflection of meaning.

According to Seidman (2013), the intent of each interview is as follows:

- Interview 1—Focused Life History: The intent is to hear as much as possible about the participant in light of the topic up to the present time. This interview will ask the participant to detail the events, which have led the participant to where they are now in their life, discussing major events that have impacted their life.
- Interview 2—The Details of Experience: The intent is to concentrate on the concrete details a participant's lived experience in the topic area using specific events that were touched upon during the first interview as ones that were to be re-constructed by the participant.
- Interview 3—Reflection of Meaning: The intent is to reflect on the meaning of the experiences and identify the intellectual and emotional connections. In the third interview, the participant is asked questions that connect the life-history, important events, and further discussion of the research topic in order to make new meaning of their experience. The third interview is one that asks the participant to creatively or critically reflect on what the research topic means to them as a human being.

Interviewing is the crux of phenomenological inquiry as it is through the language of experience, most importantly the perception of an experience, that the learners can share their lived experience. Interviews assist in helping the person recall moments in their lives where, "[t]he parts are separated in time, but linked with a common meaning, and the aim of the interview would be to recall the parts and their connections and discover this common meaning" (Smith, Flowers, & Larkin, 2009, pp. 72–73). Interviews, however, are not enough to reach the goals of research; phenomenologists believe that "access to experience is always dependent on what participants tell us about that experience, and that the researcher then needs to interpret that account from the participant in order to understand their experience" (Smith, Flowers, & Larkin, 2009, p. 75).

Data Analysis: Interpretative Phenomenological Analysis (IPA)

IPA researchers are especially interested in what happens when the everyday flow of lived experience takes on a particular significance for people. This usually occurs when something important has happened in our lives.
—Smith, Flowers, & Larkin (2009, pp. 47–48).

In phenomenology, a primary goal is in understanding the essence of an experience that is experienced by individuals, but also shared by a variety of people. In order to understand the essence of a shared experience, the collected narrative requires interpretation. I decided, therefore, to use interpretative phenomenological analysis (IPA) and the work of Smith, Flowers, and Larkin (2009), as the data analysis resource. IPA is grounded in phenomenology, as its primarily an "interpretative endeavor and is therefore informed by hermeneutics, the theory of interpretation" (Smith, Flowers, & Larkin, 2009, p. 82), which is crucial to reaching the aims of this research: to better understand the experience of the person.

Although IPA is commonly used in education scholarship, as well as other disciplines that include scholars "concerned with the human predicament" (Smith, Flowers, & Larkin, 2009, p. 118), the analysis originates in the psychology discipline. Smith (1996) in his article "Beyond the Divide Between Cognition and Discourse: Using Interpretative Phenomenological Analysis in Health Psychology Argued for an Approach to Psychology," discussed a desire to utilize qualitative lived experience data of patient perception in conversation with the more quantitative mainstream psychology scholarship. Smith, understanding the importance of the nature of perception in healing, saw a role for what was considered, at that time, subjective data in an objective data focused field.

IPA (Smith & Osborn, 2003) consists of four primary methods:

1. Locating themes within transcriptions (close-reading)
2. Clustering themes (phenomenological horizons)
3. Connecting themes with transcriptions (data coding)
4. Reflective writing (bracketing/*reductio*)

Locating Themes

In order to locate themes, IPA requires detailed transcriptions of each interview that is then pored over at length. Typically, when researchers use IPA, the text of the transcription are marked on one margin with copious notes. Smith and Osborn describe this as "free-text analysis" where the researcher makes comments as an attempt "at summarizing or paraphrasing, some will be associations or connections that come to mind, and others may be preliminary interpretations" (Smith and Osborn, 2003, p. 67). Once the researcher makes the margin notes, the transcripts are reread in order to consider how the notes and the transcriptions create potential thematic notions.

Clustering Themes (Phenomenological Horizons)

Once the themes have been located within the transcripts, they are clustered into "phenomenological horizons" (Husserl, 1913/1982) that can be described as the ecology of perception of a given topic. These horizons act as overarching umbrella constructs that are later used to guide interparticipant comparisons and are a primary step in interpreting the meaning, or essence, of an experience. These horizons are then color coded within the transcripts with color references located within the footer of the documents in order to provide an additional layer of correlation and pattern making.

Connecting Themes (Horizons) With Transcriptions

Once the horizons are created, they are categorized within tables to link directly to transcribed data (these are color coded for easy identification). In this way, the perception of the participant, based on their own use of language, is never far behind the proposed interpretation or analysis. Since the aim of phenomenology is to explore the perception of an experience with limited judgment or bias, it is important to continually reference the transcriptions so that the participants' language can ultimately live alongside the interpretation.

Reflective Writing

Interwoven with the aforementioned steps of analysis, the act of reflective writing is instrumental in the IPA practice. Not only is reflective writing a practical tool in the creation of themes and horizons, it is required as part of the "bracketing" process. According to Smith, Flowers, and Larkin, phenomenologists

> need to "bracket," or put to one side, the taken-for-granted world in order to concentrate on our perception of that world. This idea of bracketing has mathematical roots. It relates to the idea of separating out or treating separately; this is much like the contents of the brackets within equations. (Smith, Flowers, & Larkin, 2009, pp. 244–246)

Bracketing, or *reductio*, is a critical component in phenomenological analysis since it operates as the balance between the researcher and the participant; in other words, to fully explore the perceived experience of a participant, the researcher must put aside his or her judgments of the perception and stay connected to it instead. It is through the act of reflective writing that this bias is able to be identified and "set aside" so that the researcher moves from the "distraction and misdirection of their own assumptions and preconceptions, and back toward the essence of their experience of a given phenomenon" (Smith, Flowers, & Larkin, 2009, pp. 256–257).

According to Smith, Flowers, and Larkin, phenomenological studies, which use IPA, "usually have a small number of participants and the aim is to reveal something of the experience of each of those individuals. As part of this, the study may explore in detail the similarities and differences between each case" (Smith, Flowers, & Larkin, 2009, p. 92). Additionally, the intimate nature of phenomenological studies required participant selection to have careful consideration. Since I would be spending a minimum of three hours with each person (not to exceed a 10-day span), I sought out an anchor point within the established and well-respected punk organization to assist me in locating potential participants.

The first community I approached, *Razorcake*, welcomed my request not only to assist with communication, but also offered to act as a physical host for interviewing. As mentioned in previous chapters, *Razorcake*, founded in 2001, is one of the few print-based punk 'zines operating in the United States. Located in the Highland Park neighborhood of East Los Angeles, *Razorcake* has more than 1,000 individual subscribers all over the world, and also ships multiple issues to record and bookstores for distribution. Additionally, *Razorcake* donates hundreds of issues to community centers and other organizations, including the expansive Los Angeles county and city library systems with more than 150 locations.

Razorcake has a strong web presence, which includes archived electronic issues and monthly music podcasts created by *Razorcake* community contributors. The volunteer staff at *Razorcake* generously allowed me to post a solicitation on their website. During my solicitation in 2011, I received inquiries via email from 15 people who lived all over the United States. After touching base with several potential interviewees, I narrowed the scope to the regional areas that were my focus: California, Florida, Oregon, and Washington, DC; this left eight potential interviewees. At that point, I reached out to all eight to describe the interview process and time commitment, as well as the topics to be covered during the interview. After this phase of communication, I was left with six willing participants who all resided in either California or Florida and ranged in age between 30 and 45-years-old. Five identified as male and one as female; all of the participants identified as White and one additionally identified as Jewish.

Interview Protocol and Schedule

Smith, Flowers, and Larkin acknowledge that since IPA researchers "wish to analyze in detail how participants perceive and make sense of things which are happening to them. It therefore requires a flexible data collection instrument." Thus, the decision was to use semistructured interviewing that "allows the researcher and participant to engage in a dialogue, where initial questions are modified in the light of the participants' responses and the investigator is able to probe interesting and important areas which arise" (Smith, Flowers, & Larkin, 2009, p. 57).

The interview protocol (Appendix B) was inspired by Smith and Osborn (2003), who outline the goals of phenomenological in-depth interviewing as the attempt to "get as close as possible to what your respondent thinks about the topic, without being led too much by your questions" (p. 61). So as to keep to the spirit of the semistructured nature of the interviews, I created "prompts" in an attempt to ask the participant to "reconstruct" (per Seidman [2006], asking participants to reconstruct, rather than retell is an important aspect of gaining detailed narrative) storied experiences connected to punk engagement. These prompts were not meant to act as a rigid question regiment, rather they were guides to use as the interview conversation organically unfolded (Table 2.1).

The schedule of interviews for all six participants was ambitious. Each interview was ideally between 45 and 75 minutes; with each participant requiring three individual interviews, it was important that I held to all appointments. Of the six participants, three lived in the Los Angeles, California, area; I spent two weeks in Altadena, California, using *Razorcake* as my interview base where I completed my interview cycle with three male participants. The remaining three participants lived in the Gainesville, Florida, area. From start to end, all interviews (as well as their subsequent transcriptions) were completed between February 1, 2014, and March 1, 2014.

Limitations of Study

Given the desire for research to convey validity and reliability, it is important to understand the nuances of the phenomenological method of research. Phenomenology, by nature, is meant to "bring to light" (van Manen, 1990) the essence of a shared experience. The focus is meant to elucidate that which is not always easily seen; yet, the methodology does not automatically lend itself to transferability to a wide variety of people. In other words, the essence of an experience, as defined by a phenomenological study, may or may not be relevant to people beyond the participants of that specific study. The interpretations that are brought to life are meant to play a role in a larger process of self-discovery and a deeper understanding of the human experience; they are less concerned with asserting any type of finding that can be universally applied. With this in mind, the implications of phenomenological studies can manifest in a number of ways, but to stay true to its spirit, they should be intimate and personal in nature. Phenomenologists believe it is through the intimate understanding of self and others

TABLE 2.1   Interview Questions

Interview One *Focused Life History*	Interview Two *The Details of Experience*	Interview Three *Reflection of Meaning*
Please tell me a little bit about your timeline as a learner, either in school or outside of school.	Can you tell me a story that illustrated your engagement with punk that is memorable?	Tell me a bit about your current life. What does an average day look like?
How did you become to identify with a punk Community? At what age? Can you describe the life events that had led you to this community?	Please describe your definition(s) of punk Ideology/Philosophy	How do you continue to identify as punk? What does this currently look like for you?
Please tell me a bit about this initial punk community? Where was it geographically (regionally, city, rural)? How would you describe it? How would you describe the other members of this community?	Please describe your definition(s) of punk Music. What are some examples of bands that have been important to you? How? When?	In what ways do you present as punk to others? How might they "know" this aspect of your identity?
Please share some key events (related to punk) in your life since this initial involvement.	In what ways have you been a participant in either punk Ideology or punk Music? Please be specific with number of years, dates, and regional locations	Please describe the ways in which your punk involvement, to this point, has informed your current work as a learner and educator?

that societal change must ultimately originate from; therefore, research that exposes these intimate notions should be anything but disregarded.

Although I found in-depth interviewing to be highly effective in producing rich narrative data about lived experience, a layer of limitation within language exists when it is dependent on the level of honesty and self-awareness of the participant. In other words, qualitative research, specifically phenomenology-based, desires to explore the nature of being human. However, this desire can only go so far, as it is dependent on as how well a participant is able to verbally articulate their humanity (or their perception of their humanity). Even the most nuanced interpretation cannot make up for these potential chasms.

Additionally, the participants in this study are not able to represent the totality of Los Angeles, California, or Gainesville, Florida, punk communities in regards to age, ethnic/racial identity, or gender identity. The six participants can only speak to the details of their lived experience; therefore, the perception of their punk engagement is most likely informed by the ways in which they identify. As briefly discusses in the Critique of Punk section within the previous section, the nature of punk and punk ethos can be experienced very differently based on how the punk learner identifies. With this in mind, the fact that five out of six participants identified as White and male will not only influence their perception of themselves within the context of a punk community, but will also inform the ways in which they perceive others (see Duncombe & Tremblay, 2011; Nguyen, 1998; Shermer, 2004; Traber, 2001 for more on the relationship between racial identity and punk participation).

Lastly, researcher bias is an important limitation to note. During the transcription and analysis process, I engaged in the practice of "bracketing" in order to ease and manage the impacts of my bias or judgment on the data collection and interpretation; however, my bias is alive and well within the very nature of the topic I chose and the lens I choose through which to see education. My lived experience as a learner (in multiple contexts) and my participation in punk communities furthered my work (by allowing me access to insider punk communities); yet this bias also required monitoring so as not to interfere with the process. Undoubtedly, this separation of the author and learner will never be pure; however, phenomenology does not require it to be pure, rather it asks for a balance to be struck so as to honor an accurate interpretation of data.

3

Punk Learner Narrative Profiles

Illustrated by E. Bowers

Phenomenology tries to penetrate the layers of meaning of the concrete by tilling and turning the soil of daily existence.
—van Manen, 1990

As discussed in the preceding chapter, the human experience, as well as the understanding and description of that experience, is the heart of the phenomenological approach. Phenomenologists are most concerned with "what the experience of being human is *like*, in all of its various aspects, but especially in terms of the things that matter to us" (Smith, Flowers, & Larkin, 2009, p. 11). In order to best represent the lived experience that "matters," I chose to construct narrative profiles to capture both the events as they transpired for the people I interviewed, but also their interpretation and reaction to those events as they related to their education and their engagement in punk. In the previous chapters where I focused on the structure of the research, I referred to those who I interviewed as participants or interviewees; in this chapter, I intend to better honor each interviewee as a human learner. As I am no longer discussing the details of methodology and data analysis, I will now refer to each of the interviewees as *punk learners* for the remainder of the book.

Narrative Profile Creation

I would meet each punk learner at a location of their choosing, often where he or she found the most comfort—dim-lit late-night bars, southern barbecue restaurants, recently vacuumed living rooms, or citronella scented outdoor patios. During each session, there were moments of thoughtful reflection, pauses to calm crying children, opportunities to share pages from favorite books, and breaks to wipe away tears. The stories that were re-created and shared evoked an array of emotions for each of the punk learners—anger, relief, shame, doubt, frustration, sadness, joy, and pride were but a handful. Each moment documented and preserved in the interview transcripts.

All six punk learners engaged in three face-to-face interviews, with the individual interviews lasting approximately one hour. Because the stories were highly personal in nature, I was careful to participate in member checking, which is the "quality control process by which a researcher seeks to improve the accuracy, credibility, and validity of what has been recorded during a research interview" (Harper & Cole, 2012, p. 510). The acts of a qualitative researcher have the possibility of being highly exploitive in an arena that is rich with intimate stories of lived experience, and although it is was not my research design or goal to conduct purely participant constructed research, I wanted to make sure there was nothing written on behalf of any punk learner that they did not read first or agree with. It was through this member-checking process that the punk learner's voice and experience was privileged beyond any research agenda or researcher analysis.

To complete the first step of the member-checking process, I sent full interview transcriptions to each punk learner who wanted to review them (one punk learner declined to review the text) so that they could assure their words and meanings were accurately transcribed. During this step, I allowed each punk learner the freedom to delete, clarify, or expand upon the transcriptions. I told them that the transcribed story was theirs, not mine, to share, so it was crucial that it read accurately. Even though they would have had the freedom to do so, this process didn't equate into punk learners' overly editing, retracting, or concealing information. There were times when the punk learners would report that it was "awkward" to read every intimate detail that they had spoken to me; however, all punk learners verified that the text was accurate and approved it for publication.

The purpose of using phenomenological interviewing is to capture the essence of an experience through language and descriptive memory. In other words, it is important for me as a researcher to present and share not only the experience, but also the ways in which the punk learner viewed and described the experience. The punk learner's perceived reality *is* their reality (van Manen, 1990, 1995); therefore it was imperative to explicate the punk learner's perception of their lived experience in addition to the more concrete details of the experience.

Creating punk learner profiles using the transcription data allowed me to present the lived experience of each participant using their own words, and their own way of describing their experience. To accomplish this goal, in addition to member checking, I also paid particular detail to attend to the phenomenological practice of *reductio*, also known as reduction or bracketing. Reductio, specifically in terms of hermeneutic reduction (there are additional types connected to varied phenomenological methods), is concerned with the researchers ability to maintain openness. Van Manen (as cited in Friesen, Henriksson, & Saevi, 2012) describes this form of reduction as when the researcher overcomes,

> one's subjective or private feelings, preferences, inclinations, or expectations that may seduce or tempt one to come to premature, wishful, or one-sided understandings of an experience and that would prevent one from coming to terms with a phenomenon as it is lived through. (p. 25)

In other words, the phenomenologist must balance their intuitive understanding of the experienced topic, in order to uncover the essence of an experience as it is experienced; the punk learner's words and perception must not be compromised or overshadowed by the researchers own perceptions of the experience being described.

The profiles allow for the punk learner's language to live and breathe within the confines of this profile; yet the creation of the profile is a creative endeavor, as I am the one who chose the order of the text. Given that the profiles only contain approximately one-third of the transcribed narrative, I was required to use my discretion when I chose what to or what not to include. In this way, reductio was a crucial practice as I worked diligently to choose the passages that were the richest in storied detail, as well as the narratives that were the most relevant to the research questions. Overall, I wanted the passages that, when pieced together, could showcase a concise and detailed timeline of the punk learners' perception of learning and their engagement with punk rock.

I worked hard to make sure my textual choices did not become a louder voice than that of the punk learner; therefore, as a second step of member checking, acting in the service of reduction, the punk learner profile drafts were sent for a final approval. Each punk learner, again, was able to edit or delete sections of the profile to which they objected; it was imperative that each participant was comfortable with how I pieced together his or her narrative. I wanted to assure the punk learners that their story was represented in a way that was truthful and honoring. Additionally, each punk learner was offered the option of being referred to by a pseudonym; five of the six participants chose for their real names to be used.

The following pages contain the six punk learner profiles, each preceded by a researcher authored introduction; however each profile narrative uses first person language as the words are taken directly from participant interview transcripts. The profiles are also illustrated, created with the punk 'zine aesthetic in mind, in order to offer multiple modes of lived experience descriptors.

Aaron

Introduction

The first time I met Aaron, it was at his house; he welcomed me in as if we were long lost friends. Right away I was taken aback by how warm and friendly he was; we had no prior connection other than an email exchange and one mutual acquaintance, yet he treated me like family, offering me food and drink, as well as access to his home space. As I grew to know Aaron, I understood that his inviting persona was a magnet for many others as well. The one interview that took place outside of his home occurred in a local Gainesville bar; we could barely audiorecord for more than 5 minutes before being interrupted by a number of passerbys who couldn't resist giving him a hug or waving a fond hello.

Identifying as a "proud southerner," Aaron is of average height, with short dark hair; tattoos covered parts of his arms and legs. Wearing black frame glasses, he has an expressive face. Most of the time, we met at his house because the evenings were the only time when he could spare a minute: he is a new dad with twin, 10-month-old babies and so our conversations were often in between feedings, diapering, or bathing. During the interviews, there didn't seem to be any question too personal or private: Aaron often shared to a greater depth than I predicted he would be comfortable with. More than once I was humbled by Aaron's willingness to open up about his past painful memories or joyous events. During our three interview sessions together, I rarely spoke. Aaron filled the time with his overflowing memories, his raw emotions, and his intense loyal commitments. Aaron had a most real and earnest presence about him; mindful to treat me well, but not ever in the least bit shy or embarrassed for who he is or was.

Punk Learner Profile

> *And you can't say, "Well what if I wasn't into punk rock?" You can't make that kind of conjecture—because it's just so much a part of who I am—it's like asking, "What if I wasn't from West Virginia?"*
> —Aaron

My name is Aaron and I am 37-years-old. I was born in Boone County, West Virginia, but I currently live in Gainesville, Florida, and have since 1996.

When I was beginning school, my parents thought that private education equaled better education, so they put me in a private Baptist Christian school in southern West Virginia. When I started kindergarten, I remember being presented with vowels and the alphabet. I knew most of it already, so I remember being made to feel special and important. People said, "Oh Aaron, that's great that you know!" I didn't know why I knew that stuff, but my mom read to me constantly and I watched Sesame Street all the time. So those basics I knew without knowing—I remember recognizing that I had learned something without knowing that I had learned something.

Later on, my parents, through a gradual series of events, came to realize that maybe I'm not getting the best education possible. I remember that I was physically paddled in front of my peers, made to bend over the desk and paddled with a board in front of all my classmates—it was really humiliating stuff. In the third grade, my parents pulled me out because they realized I was being fed Baptist religious doctrine based on fear and far-fetched notions about everything. I started public school in the fourth grade, but I felt like an outsider.

In public school, when it came time to actually work, I didn't know how to multiply numbers and I didn't really know how to tell time on a clock. I have always struggled with math my whole life, I still do, so there was definitely attention that I needed as a young kid that I didn't get. That's when I realized that I felt like I had been cheated, so I was angry. I remembered being angry. When you are that age, you don't want to feel like an outsider—you don't want to feel stupid; I remember being made to feel that way because the kids made fun of me.

In terms of education, I think I got off to a bad start—and it was through no fault of my parents because they were always nurturing and encouraging, and they never let me forget how important school was or how important education was. My dad would say, "You don't want to be a dumbass like me." I remember my dad, and by that point he was already disabled from an accident at work in the coal mine and home all the time, sitting with me and helping me memorize my multiplication tables. He would go over my homework with me. But I don't feel like that feeling of being an outsider, especially in the school environment, ever left me.

In fifth grade, I made friends and I adjusted pretty well—I guess I was relatively popular, but I had lots of behavior problems. They kept my desk right by the teacher's desk. I was always getting in trouble—not for being a bad kid, but I couldn't sit still and I was very hyperactive. In sixth grade, we moved from West Virginia to Crystal River, Florida: one small town to another small town, but it felt like a bustling metropolis to us because it had more than one fast-food restaurant. I've always been naturally curious, so in middle school, which was the worst for so many reasons, I was still curious. In the new middle school, they thought I talked funny, they thought I dressed funny: I had a really thick Appalachian accent. I immediately stuck out, got beat up, got picked on—the teachers were checked out, you know—it sucked. I really didn't like school.

I remember I had some horrible teachers, specifically my 7th grade math teacher, Ms. Brooks. She knew that I didn't know the answer and I couldn't do the work, and she didn't like me. I know that now. She was a spiteful mean old lady and she would make me go to the board in front of all my classmates even though she knew I couldn't do the problem (Figure 3.1). I remember the very real palpable physical panic I would have. The sweating and dizzying was right out of a movie. It made me feel like, "Fuck this, fuck these teachers, I don't need

Figure 3.1 Aaron at the blackboard.

this anyway." That experience made me resent education and think negatively about school, but my parents were always like, "It's important, it's important."

By the time I got to high school, which is a whole other nightmare, it felt like the teachers were against us. It was really alienating. I became aware that I wasn't getting a good education and that my teachers were all just lackeys. There were a couple of really good ones and I don't want to throw them all under the bus, but most of them weren't: I don't know why they were teachers, I guess they were just too lazy to do anything else.

I got a job at a marina when I was 14. My uncle worked there as a boat mechanic and I got a job there before I could drive so my mom had to take me to work. I remember thinking, "I'm learning *now!*" I worked with these older guys who took me under their wing. These guys were wild rednecks, but they were good people, hard workers. They had lived a life. So I learned a great deal about life and about work ethic—the right way to be. Mostly "man stuff," I guess you could say. Ways to interact in adult situations, ways of interacting with other men.

My boss was awesome, his name was Mike O'Mellian and I remember many times, where my hyperactive, irresponsible obnoxious adolescent self would override whatever was supposed to be happening, Mike would say, "What the fuck man, you need to get your shit together!" I remember liking this guy so much that I wanted to be his equal and I wanted to impress him and do a good job. He'd say, "You know, you are really fuckin' up man, you need to get all your shit in one bucket!"—that's how he put it. I learned a lot from working at that marina in Old Homosassa, Florida. Magic Manatee Marina—it's still there. You know... there was a sign hanging on a tree that was clearly visible as you went into Old Homosassa that said, "Don't let the sun set on your black ass in Old Homosassa." Up until 1993, that sign was there—true story. I think that whole time I worked there on that marina, I saw maybe two Black folks on that river.

By the time I was in tenth grade, I thought, "I want to make good grades, I want to learn." I had begun to read a lot in order to take charge of my own learning because I was old enough to realize that my situation at the high school was bullshit. I was in a shitty school system, I had shitty teachers, I had shitty peers, I hated everyone in my high school except for a couple of people. I thought, "Hey, you are getting shafted here, you need to pay attention to the world, and you need to try to learn."

I'm not tooting my own horn, but I've always been a curious kid, the older I get the more curious I become—so I started taking charge of my own learning. This was at the same time that I became very interested in punk rock and literature—both worked in tandem. After I was deeply, deeply into punk rock and started reading Kurt Vonnegut and Jack Kerouac, I remember walking down the hall in high school with a better feeling. I felt like, "You guys are all fucking idiots and you guys are all assholes, but I know shit you don't and fuck you." I remember that it was comforting—I didn't feel as tragic anymore. I felt empowered.

Learning outside of school definitely got some traction in high school when I met Kevin. Kevin's grandfather owned the Days Inn hotel that was a mile from my house, so during the summer he would come up from Orlando to work in Crystal River at the hotel for his grandfather. I recently found a letter that he wrote me in 1995 when I was a senior in high school, it's a 7-page letter—he was living in Arizona at the time. It was amazing to read because I had forgotten the impact that this guy had had on my life. Kevin was a very smart guy—he was older than me, probably by 5 or 6 years. He had a room at the Days Inn when he was there, and he had a kick-ass stereo—and we'd listen to all this classic rock stuff, Pink Floyd and Rush and Guns N' Roses and smoke weed and get super stoned. But I remember him telling me that I shouldn't hang around with my stoner friends, "You're different from them and you are smart and you need to stop smoking so much weed and you should focus on school and you should read" and I was like, "whatever," and I definitely shrugged it off at the time.

He introduced me to a lot of things—a lot of food, a lot of art, literature, music—but more importantly than all of that, a more enlightened way of thinking about the world and people. He introduced me to the basics of Western philosophy, existentialism—through conversation and books. He helped me take the blinders off, I guess. He opened my eyes. And I know it was definitely because of him that I started considering, "Maybe I should go to college." Because before that, I never thought it was going to happen, before that I couldn't even picture living to 30. A lot of that belief goes back to when my dad got hurt when I was 5—I realized at a young age that shit happens like that. I thought that there was no need to make long-term plans and have long-term goals because I could be dead in 5 minutes. I remember thinking this at a really young age. I thought, "Wait, my dad just went to work and now he is never going to walk again."

My independent learning progressed in high school—and I think beyond high school. Punk and independent learning became almost synonymous because literature and punk were and are so similar. When I moved to Gainesville after high school, I moved from an environment where nobody read, nobody talked about books. If you were smart, you were weird. The people in my Crystal River high school called you a fag if you were an intellectual or an artist. I remember moving to Gainesville and realizing that I was surrounded by interesting and smart people. And everyone was into music—punk rock and hip-hop and metal. I remember I'd go to someone's house and they would have bookshelves and records and I remember it just being so new to me. It was an immensely positive thing, but foreign, completely foreign.

I have always been fascinated by music. When I was a little kid going to church, about once a month, the church service would reach a fever pitch. Everyone would get in their cars and drive down to Little Coal River, which is a brown, muddy river that runs through Boone County. I remember being a little kid and watching these people in their Sunday best wade in the water—the preacher would be waist deep in the water and he would have a Bible in one hand (Figure 3.2). He would be preaching and dunk them under the water to baptize them. On the bank there would be a guy picking the guitar—looking back and hearing that instrument—hearing these acoustic instruments on the riverbank. I remember being a little kid and being fixated on that. To this day, when I hear Appalachian music, bluegrass, whatever you want to call it—when I hear those instruments being played—I can hear it all day, listen to it all day long.

It was sixth grade when I first discovered punk rock. Before that I would just dig through my dad's tapes. In West Virginia I had an older neighbor and his parents didn't know he had Motley Crue tapes and KISS tapes and Ozzy tapes, but he had them and it was definitely an illicit thing. I was still super into heavy metal when I moved to Florida in 1987, but then I met this kid who gave me a copy of a copy of a copy of a tape—it was the Dead Milkmen's first record *Big Lizard in My Backyard*. Up to that point, all the music I had heard was metal.

Figure 3.2 Preacher in the river.

I remember hearing this Dead Milkmen record—here are these songs about doing laundry and about hating going to the beach and how you love it when your girlfriend cooks swordfish—and I could tell that these were just normal dudes making music. I didn't understand it all and I didn't necessarily like it at first. I was like, "What the fuck is this?" It didn't compute at all. I remember having the tape for a while—it wasn't like I liked it or didn't like it, I just didn't know what to make of it. Obviously there was no Internet so I couldn't look it up—I didn't know Dead Milkmen. I didn't know where they were from, who they were, or whatever. I didn't know they were four adolescents from Philadelphia. I ended up falling madly in love with this record and listened to it over and over and over. It remains one of my favorite records of *any* genre to this day.

At that same time, I was starting to question things about the world and be somewhat aware about politics—and I'm seeing all these things pop up in the music I'm listening to—and that was one of the things I loved about punk rock—it could be totally ridiculous, funny and in jest, you know? Like there are songs about doing laundry, but then there are also songs about Cambodia—and I was like, "Where is Cambodia? What the fuck is going on in Cambodia?"

The first time I went to Gainesville, I think I was 14—that was when I really caught the punk rock bug. I went to my first Radon show at the Hardback with my buddy who had a learner's permit (Figure 3.3). The Hardback was a tiny bar and then outside it was just a big empty warehouse. Radon played on the fucking floor. Even though I had heard punk rock, I didn't know that's how it existed. I didn't know it existed in that fashion.

Figure 3.3 Aaron at the Hardback.

"Is that violence? No that's dancing." And every time someone falls down, somebody picks them up and there are people crowding around the singer screaming the words into the microphone. Their arms are around each other and everyone is smiling and grinning and singing. I remember having the thought that I wanted to be on *that* team, I wanted to be on that side—that's *my* team.

I remember very vividly that my eyes were like saucers—half scared and terrified because I had never seen dudes with purple hair and bolts through their noses—I mean there were definitely some stereotypical punk rock looking dudes there at the time—stinky dudes in leather jackets and mohawks, and I had never seen that before—all with tattoos you know? As weird as everybody looked to me, it felt fucking awesome. I mean everything I can think to say sounds cliché, but I knew I wanted to be a part of it for sure—for the first time in my life, I felt totally affirmed.

I was so alienated in my own surroundings in Crystal River and so it was a very empowering feeling—punk rock hit all the points. It was funny sometimes, it was clever sometimes, it was informative, and it was even sometimes contradictory. I didn't understand it, I don't claim that I ever did completely understand it—that was one of the things that was mysterious about it, but I knew it was music and art being made by smart people. I started going to record stores where I could buy a 7-inch for two bucks. Or I could go to shows and people would *give* me 7-inchs. It was so exciting to my teenage brain. I thought that was so cool—I mean I'm holding this 7-inch record and that band just got the money together and they made this fucking record themselves. They recorded it, they sent it off and had it made. They screen printed their own covers and they gave me one!

I remember walking through my high school after I had gotten into punk rock and I started reading books—I felt so empowered—and even though I didn't have anybody to share it with really, I felt like I was in on something that was really special and that I was in on something that was better than all the assholes I went to school with. It definitely made being smart cool. Punk told me that knowledge was a good thing.

You can't use the term punk and have it just mean one thing—there are so many different definitions. Many different bands with different styles and different deliveries of what they were doing with their art. Even the stuff that you could call stupid or mindless was still clever. There was still something, I saw something in it—and it encouraged me to know that even when you are being silly, you are not being stupid and you're not being ignorant or being blind. That's something, you know? Because I just felt like I was in such a vapid environment in Crystal River—like there was just no substance to anything or anyone. I felt that way then, and I feel that way now. You know I hated pop music, I hated sports, and I hated my teachers—but it all sort of blended together to be the same shit that I hate *now* as a 37-year-old man—subservient mediocrity. You know, bad art, bad food, bad company, bad jokes, bad humor—like subpar America. Punk rock was the antithesis of that. It was anything *but* subpar.

When I go to shows these days, and just seeing Radon the other night was a perfect example, it was beautiful, it was wonderful. Some of these songs—two in particular—it's hard not to weep because it just evokes so many memories and emotions. My point is, I'm standing there at 37 and the first time I saw this band, I was 14. Seeing this band playing these songs, it still passionately moves me.

If you are a guy or girl that ever put on the Misfits when you were 13 or 14 and it set you on fire and you loved it, I think you are just a passionate person anyway—you are moved by things. I know that when I am an old man and someone puts on "Bullet" by the Misfits, for example, I'm going to be like "Oh yeah, this is a great song." It's hard to imagine growing out of that—I guess it goes back to that feeling of belonging that affirms the things you like and don't like about the world around you—and I don't think you ever stop liking that spirit.

For the record, I'm not one of these banner-waving punks; I don't often talk about punk rock as a set of ideals. I love punk rock, but I don't even listen to it that much anymore and I listen to music every day, all day. However, I just turned 37 and I know that when I'm an old, old man, I will always know that the sweetest and greatest things that I have in my life and gotten to experience in my life, have been directly linked to punk rock. For sure—without question. Everything that I've done, everything that I champion—there is no way it can be understated.

Yam

Introduction

I met with Yam in the basement of the organization where he works. Tall and thin, with black wavy hair, Yam has a very reserved and quiet presence. Yam looks a touch younger than his age, with light facial hair and glasses, he exudes an approachable and kind energy. His answers to questions are sometimes pensive, as if he is unsure how to respond—or if he wants to respond at all. Yam allows for a significant pause in between a questions and his answer; when he would respond with an even tone and flow, his words would cut right to the heart of what he wanted to say. Yam wouldn't hesitate to share a love or distaste for an experience or person.

Yam rarely showcased any joyful responses or laughs at his own stories, but at times, he would shyly smile with an almost embarrassed look—as if I was asking him to betray a secret. During our conversation, he had a consistent restrained demeanor that could have been interpreted as distant or removed from our conversation, as if he were somewhere else in a daydream; yet he returned to each interview with an increased sense of vibrancy and investment in the process. During our last interview, when I asked him to tell me about a few moments on his band's last tour, Yam showcased great elation and nostalgia while re-creating the experience—this was an atypical response, which left me feeling fortunate to have seen an excitable part of his persona.

Punk Learner Profile

> *Punk is an introduction to the idea of radical ideas.*
> —Yam

My friends call me Yam. I am 30-year-old. From when I was born until right before kindergarten, I lived in the San Fernando Valley—a suburb of Los Angeles. When I was 5, we decided to move to the Santa Clarita Valley, which is the next suburb—10 or 15 miles from the city. I lived there until my second year of college. For the past 10 years, I have lived in Los Angeles.

My mom is a preschool teacher and my father is a junior high science teacher. They have had those jobs my entire life, so education was always really important for *them*, but I always hated school and never really appreciated it or enjoyed it. I actually don't have any memories of my life where I wasn't in some kind of school. I started going to preschool at 12 months when my mom went back to work, so for the first 22 years of my life, school was the main thing that I did. My mentality has always been: *I have to get done with school—my goal is to be done with school forever.*

If I wasn't doing well in school, which would be quite frequently, my dad would say to me, "This is your job. You have to do good at school." So I thought about school like a job, but it was a job that I didn't want. There was just so much busy work that was constantly being put upon me to complete and I thought that there was just no reason to do it. Despite my feelings about school, it was always possible enough to get decent grades, enough to get by, but I never really found school all that fun, with few exceptions.

Looking back, I've forgotten everything other than basic math and maybe some geometry; I question if any of it is really worth it.

Year after year, I would get put in the dumb kid class, where crowd control is more important than teaching. I think so many teachers are just there because they need the money and end up doing a subpar job because they don't actually care about teaching. In the dumb kid class, I'd get straight A's and then be put into a more advanced class, but then not get good grades there and then get put back. I mean between third, fourth, fifth, and sixth grades, I feel like I got put back and forth between those two and everyone knew what class was what. They knew if they were in the smart kid class or if they were in the underachiever class.

In terms of learning, I always enjoyed looking at maps. I remember I spent a lot of time not paying attention in class because I was looking at the maps that were in the back of my textbooks (Figure 3.4). Fourth-grade history was the first subject I remembered caring about; my teacher would lend me history books—he'd bring the books to school from his home and I would read them.

The history covered in those books were the realest thing I read about in school—I mean the history they usually teach kids in school is so glossed over and played out and safe compared to what it really was—the books he lent me showed something that was gritty and different. I was most

Figure 3.4 Yam looking at maps.

interested in the books on WWII and the Holocaust. Maybe I was so interested because I'm Jewish and this is the first time Jewish people are being brought up in class; in my school, I remember, there weren't many other kids in the school who were Jewish.

While I was not paying attention in class, I would always do artistic work. I would just constantly draw or doodle. I would fill endless notebooks full of drawings, but you wouldn't see any development of any type of artistic skill—just constant pen on paper drawing people and words. There weren't a lot of other things I was interested in, but I definitely learned a lot of useless information from television. At one time, the majority of stuff I knew might have been learned from school, but now I think that equally, if not more, is the stuff I learned from TV.

As I saw it, the main priority of my high school was football and so that was kind of the level that everybody was at. Everyone was just racist, homophobic—just like shitty people. I was happy when I left and went to a different school during my junior year. For the first time, the classrooms weren't full of shitty people; they were pretty interesting people and not hateful. I could connect with the teachers and actually have discussions. I was almost done with high school, but it was the first time I felt like I had a voice in school.

In terms of my learning style, the idea of taking a history class or a philosophy class—well, I guess I liked the idea of it, but I don't think I ever actually learned anything. I would just study for the test. I've come to terms with the fact that I like *doing* stuff—I mean I'd volunteer at various places and then I'd feel like I was learning more about what I *wanted* to learn. So instead of taking a sociology class, I'd rather volunteer at a food bank or something. I had to tell a bunch of people this about me—I had to explain this to my parents multiple times.

The first time I listened to punk rock was in fourth grade, 1993, the same year my teacher brought me Holocaust books from his home. That may be a coincidence, I don't know. In 1993, I wanted to get my hands on a lot of music, so I think I did the Columbia House 16 CDs for a penny three different times. I had all this new music—Green Day and Rancid and Rage Against the Machine. I loved that music, but I don't think I really thought about it as punk until I was in ninth grade, which would have been 1998. It was then, through punk music, that I became very inspired.

Going into high school, I felt that people were becoming more and more of who they were going to be as an adult. Some kids were becoming bigger assholes and other kids were saying, "I don't want to be an asshole." I saw myself as someone who was more, "I don't want to be an asshole." It was around this time that I first heard the punk band Dillinger Four—their lyrics broke walls down for me. I already knew that punk was political, but now I was starting to understand that it wasn't only about raising your fist and waving a flag, but it was also thinking, "I'm not going to give in." Dillinger Four helped me understand that it was important to have strong personal and political convictions.

While I was in high school, I had older friends who were living in the Bay area—they were a huge influence on me because they were involved with Food Not Bombs and other punk activism. I enjoyed traveling up and visiting them because where I lived, we were just sitting in the suburbs *talking* about that stuff. We would hang out with them and be around all these people that were actually being productive and doing things that were great for the community, and they were also having fun doing it. I had known one of those kids before he had moved up there and now he was a very different person, he was changing.

After high school, I really came to understand that the essence of punk is equality, open self-expression, and to help other people express themselves. Punk helped me understand that it was okay to be yourself—to understand that we are all doing what we can and we all have to get by somehow. It was at the same time that I started to create...because all of a sudden I felt that I *could* create. Punk told me that even though I wasn't in this flashy band and I wasn't this high profile person, I could still set up shows and create 'zines...I could contribute.

My wife and I were in a band for 5 years with another guy, but he recently signed to a major label with his other band. We decided we couldn't keep doing our old band together, so we started a two-piece band where I play guitar, she plays drums and we both sing (Figure 3.5). We release our own records—we don't really approach other record labels to release stuff for us, we feel more comfortable doing it ourselves. We released our first record with money that we got from our families when we got married; it's a large part of our relationship.

I believe that punk is about productivity and doing things that require as little environmental energy and resources as possible. It also should be accessible and affordable—which is another form of access I guess. In my life now, I try to never leave that train of thought. I'm always in a band, always working on a 'zine—I struggle to set up shows any way I can. I'm doing what I want to do now, what I've always wanted to do; and once I was done with school, I knew I could focus all my energy on it. I mean I am doing exactly what I've always wanted.

Figure 3.5 Yam and his wife.

Sean

Introduction

Connecting with Sean meant being flexible around his teaching schedule. As a first-year tenure track professor, Sean worked well into the evening each day, so this meant that we would spend our time together at a bar or restaurant in the midst of the small town Ventura nightlife. Sean is thin and tall, with short blonde hair and kind, soft eyes—he has a casual and light air about him that makes you feel immediately at ease.

During our interviews, Sean would often take the opportunity to profess about his ideals, about his work in the world, about his convictions. He never stumbled for an answer, always quick with a detailed and rich response. At times he was incredibly giving of his emotional memories, other times he would focus on an intellectual analysis of his life. Sean's voice is not in the least bit authoritative or demanding of attention, yet his calm and matter of fact demeanor required that his words be attended to. Sean was at times direct in his answers, and other times his words would weave in and out of philosophical pathways until he would ultimately end at his final destination.

During the time when we were preparing or ending our recordings, Sean would take the opportunity to talk about his passion for literature—his favored authors and texts—describing himself as a scholar of Thomas Pynchon. It was clear that he was a man committed to engaging with his field of expertise—he was invested in his world exactly in the ways he had imagined it to be created. Often laughing during his sharing of stories, it appeared as if he was really laughing at the cleverness of the world and the ways we all choose to live out our own realities.

Punk Learner Profile

> *What I learned from punk is the same thing I learned from Thoreau. Live life deliberately.*
> —Sean

My name is Sean and I am an English professor in my 40s. I live in Ventura, California, and have lived in California for the last couple of decades. I am originally from central Florida where I grew up in a working-class neighborhood in the late-1970s and early-80s.

I remember being a little kid and my mom taking me to the library. Going to the library was kind of a big thing because we didn't really have anything else around the house to entertain us except for books. We had a TV, but it didn't always work—it was the swamps of Florida, and so we only had three channels. My mom would take us to the library and show us how to find books—then she would let us look. I remember being on my own looking through all the aisles and I found books on the TV show "Our Gang." These books were more interesting to me than the TV show ever was.

I know this dates me a little bit, but when I was growing up, TVs had picture tubes and our picture tube was always going out. When we watched TV, it would take a while to warm up; it would be green and you couldn't really see it. We didn't have cable so it was only antenna, and the picture would come in and out. It was just a pain in the ass to try to watch something that wasn't coming in. But when you read something and you imagined it, then it's in your mind and its vivid—it's there. My imagination worked so much better than the TV did. I wasn't just like this about TV shows—I read a ton about baseball when I was a kid, but I didn't like watching baseball and I didn't particularly like playing baseball. But I loved listening to it on the radio or reading about it, and I think it was just because I could imagine everything. When I would listen to games on the radio, I would picture the players and, as a kid, I'd picture my friends out there instead of the actual players (Figure 3.6).

In the elementary school where I went, I was way ahead of my class. I was bored and could usually teach myself the lessons pretty quickly; so I was

Figure 3.6 Sean imagining baseball.

just stuck in school for the rest of the day waiting for everyone else to catch up. I remember this feeling a lot in school—this feeling that I would try to learn things on my own first and then I would just sit in class and be bored. When I was bored, I did a lot of writing—short stories, fiction. I remember feeling disconnected from the rest of my class.

It was one of those educational systems where they teach to the lowest performing kid in the class and if you're not low performing then what do you do in class? You just kind of sit there. Which is, I think, maybe what schools predominantly teach kids. They tell kids to "Get here on time, sit down and shut up. Do whatever work and when you are done doing your work don't bother me and I'll clock out at the end of the day." Especially in working class schools they have that factory mindset of the 70s. So that was my experience in elementary school and junior high. In all honesty, that was high school, too. Most of my learning during those times was done outside of school. It felt that if I wanted an education, then I had to do it myself. A lot of my education K through 12 was taking it upon myself to educate myself about the things I was interested in.

A lot of Florida schooling in the 70s and in the 80s, too, was very much about standardized testing. The thing is that standardized testing is a formula; I could probably pass multiple choice tests even if I knew nothing about a subject, because they follow a pattern (Figure 3.7). There's two possible answers, two ridiculous ones, and you just guess between the two and you will probably do okay. I mean it was just such a fucking waste of time. When in life do you ever do a multiple-choice test? When are you ever

Figure 3.7 Sean looking at a test.

faced with a problem that you are then given four options, but only one of them is right?

I remember those reading comprehension tests where they picked the most boring articles to see if you can find a word and then define it in context. Even as big of a reader as I was, that type of reading comprehension seemed like, "How well can you stay awake through this incredibly boring article and then say four *obvious* things about it." I mean I just hated that. I hated that stuff. Even as a 9-year-old, I think I could just see that it was a waste of my time, but it was the whole focus of my education.

I started working construction when I was 13 and I did it, in part, because my dad was a contractor and he would need little jobs done. On weekends, he'd say something like, "There's a pallet of blocks right here, it needs to be over there," or "Carry those blocks from over there to here," or "There's a slab here and it shouldn't be here. Get a jackhammer and hammer that slab and put all the rocks over there." He trusted me, he would say, "If you don't know how to do something, figure it out!" I probably learned more from construction as a kid than I ever did in school. I'm very academic, I mean I'm a professor now, so I'm very academic minded, but I just had better teachers on the construction sites. My involvement with punk rock was very gradual. I started listening to punk rock music when I was 15 or 16. I wasn't really involved with the punk rock scene; it was just a matter of music filtering down. So I listened to the Dead Kennedys and a few other punk bands like that.

When I was 15, I would go over to my friend's house and we would always tape *120 Minutes* on MTV—that's where we'd learn about punk bands and bands that were marginally punk... like the Pixies. I was really big into the Pixies in my adolescence and bands like them. So even though I'd listen to punk all the time, I didn't yet have a concept of punk rock as a formed community. I remember I had a Sex Pistols cassette, but I didn't know who the Sex Pistols were; I just thought they had a funny name.

My concept of punk changed when I was a student at Florida State University, I hung out with a lot of people that worked at the college radio station or were in bands. I wasn't in a band and I didn't work at the college radio station, but I would try to do some similar things with books and literature since that was my passion. I tried a couple of times to set up a reading series in Tallahassee and I would always try to write about the punk shows that I would go to. A friend of mine worked at Kinko's and we made little punk 'zines that we passed out. I would always listen to punk music at the music store and I would know everyone there.

At that time, I lived in a duplex and the head of the college radio station lived next door to me, so we shared a porch. She'd always tell me about new bands and she turned me on to new music; basically the house where I lived was the campus radio station house so I knew the punk community that way. When I'd go out to punk shows, I'd know everyone at the show. Those years were 1989 to 1992 so it wasn't a big point for new punk rock in Florida—this was kind of a valley—so there was still a lot of people that were listening to the 80s stuff—I mean a lot of what we were listening to would be the Minutemen or X or Fugazi or Minor Threat or Dead Kennedys.

When I was in my graduate program in Arizona, punk ideology hit me hard and it informed my education more than anything else. To me, punk was about getting out there and being involved, doing something. Don't sit at home and complain. *Don't get bored*—go out and create! I know a lot of time punk rock kids will push it and go out and destroy, which I guess is sometimes the fun of it, but mostly the whole idea was *be active* (Figure 3.8). In terms of punk learning in graduate school, it wasn't just about taking initiative in our classes, but it was about knowing that if you are really going to understand literature, if you are really going to understand writing, if you are really going to understand fiction—you have to go and *engage with it*.

So after I received my PhD and when I got on the tenure track at Channel Island, I knew I could actually be deliberate about curriculum. Now I can take some of these ideas from punk rock and bring them into my

Figure 3.8 Don't get bored.

classes. I didn't want them to be too dogmatic—I didn't want them to be intrusive—but rather, I wanted them to help empower kids. I think that punk values are good values for kids. I mean, I started a publishing company as a construction worker—that's about as DIY as it gets. I didn't know anything about publishing, but I figured, "Fuck, do it yourself! You want to know how to publish? Go to the library and get a book and learn how to publish!"

I believe that the DIY punk community is about creating your own culture, don't consume someone else's culture—don't just take the shit that is sold to you or just dropped in your lap—go out and make it. Make it organically and meaningful for you. I think that matches what I sought out in education, which is: Life is your search for meaning, for enrichment, so make sure to live an enriched life. This is your life—*live in a full way.*

Erin

Introduction

When I first communicated with Erin, she was driving from San Francisco to Gainesville, Florida—returning home from time spent in art school. When we finally met after she settled in at home, she humbly showed me her extensive portfolio of artistic work—incredibly detailed ink-on-paper portraits and sceneries. Erin is tall with long flowing dirty blonde hair; she has a joyous presence, which is characterized by a youthfully round face, a warm smile and welcoming disposition. Casual in clothing and hairstyle, she exudes both grace and awkward mannerisms; sometimes brimming with confidence and other times nervous with doubt. Our interview sessions fit within the few spare hours Erin has during the week—between her two jobs and her community commitments, she is often running from one thing to the next. Despite her busy schedule, we managed to spend time at one of Gainesville's busiest restaurants; during our interview, several people stopped by our table to wish Erin a happy birthday. The week before, she had turned 30—her friends had thrown her a large surprise party at a downtown bar where several local bands played.

With a light-hearted air about her, Erin is vulnerable in her responses to interview questions. At times, it appears that she is talking about her life for the first time—sometimes expressing hesitancy or confusion about the way to describe events. Other times, she overflowed with emotion—often apologizing for tearing up while she discussed painful memories. Erin engaged patiently and thoughtfully with each question—and I was consistently impressed with her dedication to share her story despite the apparent grief and sadness that surfaced at times.

Punk Learner Profile

> *I learn so much more from this life than I was ever able to learn in a classroom, perhaps because I never quite felt like myself or felt safe there. I need a good punk or DIY scene around me to live the life I want to live.*
>
> —Erin

My name is Erin and I am 30-years-old. I grew up in a small rural town in northern Florida. I recently spent time in California while I was attending art school, but I currently reside in Gainesville, Florida.

As long as I can remember, I've always drawn. When I was really young, like three or four, I would draw scenes from movies—I would make really detailed scenes. When I started to get positive feedback from people about my drawing, or when people were surprised that I could draw that well, that's when I knew that I could figure things out for myself. I could take a thought, that was mine, and I could execute it in a way that I wanted to (Figure 3.9). I think that's my original attachment to drawing—it is something that nobody taught me—I just figured it out myself.

Thinking of drawing, in this way, is funny to me because it speaks to my time in school and my relationships with teachers. I have been a pretty stubborn student, but I am also a very curious person—I'm always trying to teach myself new things every day and trying to learn for myself. I have not always been very good about learning from teachers—I'm not always good

Figure 3.9 Erin as a young artist.

at learning what I am supposed to. I had an, "I'm doing *this*!" attitude. Sometimes I was rebellious about it, but sometimes I was just clueless about it too—I was sort of day-dreamy and I was off in my own mind all the time growing up.

I grew up in a super, super, small town—I didn't even live *in* town—I grew up on a farm outside of town. I had a huge family that lived in Gainesville, but when I was at home, I was really isolated. Even though I had my sister and parents, and my grandparents lived on the other side of the farm, there was still a lot of alone time for me. I don't necessarily think that was a bad thing—I think it was really good for my imagination. Being alone allowed me to figure things out for myself and entertain myself. Even when I would be around my family or when I was around big groups of people, I just sort of wanted to go draw. I remember that when I would be in town with my huge family, my mom would say that she would find me in a closet just reading or drawing. When I was young, I would escape into reading so I never rebelled against any education that involved reading.

I think that excelling at creative things set me apart in elementary school. In my small town, it was really country and kind of backwoods. Most of the kids there had rough backgrounds. My family certainly didn't have any money, but education was really valued by my mother—both my parents cared so much. They wanted us to have all the best education wise; we didn't have any money—but they figured we could have that.

I was in the gifted program at my elementary school, which was always taught by the art teacher—so when I got taken out of my regular class and went to the art room. They would always pull me out of math—I'm still horrible at math. I would spend most of my time in elementary school in the art room, which was really good for me creatively, but I don't know if it set me up to do well in the rest of my schooling. I think teachers in elementary school treated me extra special because I was good at art and I was smart. My learning style was just doing what I wanted to do or what I thought was interesting. That initial freedom fostered my dreaminess. I expected I would have that same learning freedom when I went to middle school and high school, but it was not like that at all.

Later on, I had so many difficulties when I went to school in Gainesville, in town, because I wasn't really equipped to do the regular schoolwork. For the most part I did fine on middle school tests and what not, but when I had to focus on the work of classes, that's when I was kind of lost—that's when I went downhill school-wise.

I remained in the gifted program all through elementary school and middle school ... and most of high school as well. I got kicked out of the gifted program in high school because I skipped school too much and my grades were horrible. By the time I got to high school, I didn't really care that much about school. The me that wanted to do whatever I wanted turned defiant; rather than just being an over-imaginative kid, I was now being a bad kid.

Waldo, where I grew up, only had an elementary school. The closest middle school and high school were in this town Hawthorne—and that's where I was zoned to go to school. It's sad, because those schools were not the best place to go. Both my parents worked in Gainesville, so my mom had to petition the school board so that my sister and I could go to Gainesville schools. We ended up going to this school called Lincoln for middle school—I was there the first year of their magnet program for sixth graders. The accelerated magnet program was in a separate hallway—we almost never had classes with kids from the rest of the school—that's when I really started understanding separateness in schooling; it bothered me.

When I had been in the elementary school gifted program, I wasn't completely closed off from every other kid I went to school with. But the middle school program was in a different hallway and it was strange to know that I was in a part of the school that the rest of the school really hated. Kids in my magnet program were like, "Oh, we don't go down *that* hallway." I would have my art classes in hallways that my regular classes weren't on—we would get beat up there all the time. I think that's really when I started understanding privileged people having better classrooms because the hallways that my friends were scared to walk down were underprivileged classrooms. I remember kids from the regular program getting in trouble for being in our hallway—they were causing a ruckus or something. I remember that event really bothered me—this was around the time when I started getting really jaded with school. I didn't want to be part of something like that. I was already starting to be a bad kid and I decided I didn't want to go to school anyway.

This experience continued into my high school as well. I was in an International Baccalaureate (IB) program in a separate hallway, separate classrooms—and I eventually got kicked out because my grades were so bad. Ironically, I was still in honor classes or advanced placement classes with the other kids and I loved it. I still think it's strange—to have programs like IB where they are so separate. I mean I got kicked out, but I'm not saying that because I didn't do well, I just think it is strange to have separate programs in the same school. A lot the kids in the IB program didn't seem to have any real opinions—some of them were creative, but the rest of them just cared about grades—they would be stressed. When I went to honors classes, the kids had actual opinions and varied backgrounds, it was so much more interesting for me to go to those classes and talk with those kids.

In high school, I was really jaded. I had a ton of parent–teacher conferences because I had horrible relationships with most of my teachers—they were terrible. I remember wishing my drama teacher or my studio art teacher would have come to the conferences to tell my parents what I was *good* at. I asked myself, "Why aren't my art teachers here?" but I don't think it was an issue with particular subjects, I think it was the personalities of teachers that I would struggle with. Teachers who I thought were hard asses and that I didn't think that I would learn anything from, I would completely shut down with them. But if I was good at the work in the class, I would keep going.

Even though I had some really special teachers, I mostly remember that I had a lot of teachers in high school tell me that I wasn't even smart enough to go to community college. They would throw stuff in my face like, "If you don't finish this program, you are going to work at McDonalds" or "You'll be poor." They *didn't* say, "You will feel less fulfilled if you don't go to college." Instead, it was always, "You'll be one of those shitty kids who go to class in the other hallway. You don't want to be like the bad kids." These ideas would make me so angry (Figure 3.10). They hurt my feelings, but they also made me angry because the examples of what *not to be* were of people who were living lives they couldn't help.

Figure 3.10 Erin in school.

The teachers I had, instead of offering tutoring or helpful ways—or instead of saying, "Maybe you should go to the school counselor," they would just berate me. I had an environmental science teacher that told me that every time I came to class, he knew how much I didn't care. I had a really strict chemistry teacher—I had messed up some homework and I was trying to talk to her about it, and she was like "I know you are just a liar"—she had heard from my 10th-grade teachers about me—and she was like, "I know that you are bad." I felt like, "Shit, man, this is every class I go to."

I don't think you should say that stuff to kids at school. They would say, "I know you don't give a shit, I know you don't care about this, you are just here because you have to be here." When you tell kids stuff like that, when you tell them that they aren't going to go to college, or that they won't amount to anything—or that they are just fucking up all the time, it makes a difference. It just made me want to stop going. I was just like, "Well, fuck it—I don't want to go to school anymore."

After eleventh grade, classes were getting harder. People would ask, "Where are you going to go to college?" and there was all that pressure. Then I got my driver's license. I would go to school every once in a while, but I definitely skipped school any time I had a test or any time anything was due. I could not be persuaded that doing my schoolwork was a good idea—I think I was just pissed. It was really frustrating to be bad at stuff—or to seem like you don't get it. I wasn't used to doing bad at school because I had always done really well when I was young. I got behind, I got frustrated, I got angry—and then I just didn't go anymore. Looking back, it seems like a natural progression of just giving up.

It chips away at your confidence when people think you are bad—it makes you believe you don't deserve to try harder or to want something. I don't think I started out bad; I do think I'm pretty stubborn and I think I can be pretty indignant, but it's not hard to convince me to work hard. When I was growing up, everybody told me how smart I was all the time—how special I was—but then when you find out that you are not really good at algebra... I just didn't know how to ask for help. I hadn't had to before. I would just be failing horribly and my parents would never know—I would never tell anyone that I was doing badly. It made me feel ashamed to not do well.

My skipping school had me hanging out at the record store and stuff, so that's how I got into knowing punk kids and music—I started thinking *that* was something I wanted to be a part of. Whenever I was skipping by myself, I would drive all over Florida—or if there was any nature I wanted to see. I would figure out how far I could drive and still be home in time to not get in trouble, even though I was probably sunburned or really dirty from hiking or swimming because I always really cared about being outside. Friends that I had gone to marine biology camp with would skip school and we would go to the beach and swim; we would look for specimens. Whatever I was doing, I was mostly trying to avoid going home so I wouldn't be asked about school.

I honestly don't know how I ended up graduating from high school; we always joke that my mom paid someone—we don't actually know if she did or not. It took my parents until 2 years ago to understand that I might do things differently than they do. They are awesome people, but I think they were just ill equipped to deal with anything different than what they thought parenting would be—or what they thought parenting *should* be. They figured that if they went to work, went to church, and tried really hard, then their kids would be exactly what they wanted them to be. They couldn't figure out why that wasn't working—that maybe God had forsaken them. Even then, I always kept telling them, "I'm going to figure it out." It was really hard for them to get used to having a kid that had trouble with stuff. They weren't mad at me about it, but I think it was hard for them.

When I was young and first into punk, my involvement was based on a lot of the partying, but the music was hugely important to my artistic process—and the DIY values were always there, even if they were not always at the forefront of my mind or actions. In Gainesville, there were three places where I would see the punk shows that really shaped me: Common Grounds, Wayward Council and the Ark. The local Florida bands that meant a lot to me were FIYA, Nervous Dogs, Radon, Grabass Charlestons (now known as the Careeners), and Holopaw. I was also really into Jawbreaker and Husker Du. During that time, Riot Grrl was hugely important to me because it embodied music, performance, art, zines, and activism—it shaped a lot of my early punk values.

One of the most defining moments for me was when my friends in FIYA asked me to create the artwork for a band shirt. Even though I loved going to see them play, it was then that I sat down and *really* listened to them. That band changed my life in the sense that this band that I respected so much were my friends and were accessible to me, but were also blowing my mind with their songs. It was important for me to create for them; it was the first work I did for a band that I thought was legitimate—it made me feel legitimate.

In the DIY punk community, there were never times when I felt that there was no one there for me. There was never anyone making me feel bad about myself—or making me doubt myself. No one at a punk show would ever say, "Oh, you are really screwing up your life." So it was comforting to be with those kinds of people and make those friends—some of it may have held me back some, but I feel like it also built this beautiful life for me. I get to live here in Gainesville—all of my friends are still very close and I get to be part of this community where I can be an artist. I can be involved in community things I want to be involved.

Looking back, I have often escaped from school or family problems into my punk artist life, but that is the life that feeds me and protects me. Our community provides us with new music and art—it literally feeds us all through gardens and farms planted around town, and it gives us a safety network for when the world outside weighs on us. While I'm doing for someone else, there are people doing things for me that will make my life better.

I much prefer the idea of living in a community I helped shape and foster, to living in a world where I do what people expect and where I end up feeling so isolated and that I'm just wasting away. My friends are all doing things that I am excited about and I get to be a part of that. Whereas I never knew where I fit in at school—I was like, "I don't really know what I'm doing here," but when I am with my community here it makes sense to me. It's empowering (Figure 3.11).

Figure 3.11 Erin as grown punk artist.

Dave

Introduction

I first heard Dave's voice through my speakers years before I ever met him; as one of the singers of the punk band, Grabass Charlestons. Dave has been a long-standing member of Gainesville's DIY punk community. The interview sessions with Dave occurred during times and at locations conducive to his parenting and work schedule. As a new father, Dave creatively balances working at No Idea Records and caring for his young daughter, so I was more than humbled when he agreed to commit his time to complete our rounds of interviews.

Dave is slight in stature with serious eyes, a light beard, and long brown hair tied back in a rubber band. His reserved manner coupled with a thoughtful and deep voice allowed for relaxed casual conversation. Dave answered all the interview questions with an earnest effort to recall and recreate his life events. As we spoke, he described his life in northern Florida with sweet nostalgia—detailing poignant moments in time with friends and family, as well as relaying a deep love for the natural landscapes. His voice lifted with excitement, as he would describe the ways in which he thrived in some environments—elementary school, his first year of college, road trips, Boy Scouts. During other moments, Dave was detailed in his descriptions of life transitions—whether it be connected to his religious upbringing or his understanding of governmental systems, Dave was not hesitant to explore the times in his life when his own opinions and thoughts conflicted with the norm. Overall, Dave relayed an intense optimism in his stories—and appeared greatly fulfilled by a music community that fed his intellectual and emotional needs.

Punk Learner Profile

> *People would hand me flyers for punk shows—it felt like a gesture of acceptance. Being recognized by someone that walks the same sidewalks that I do—I knew they were on to something great.*
>
> —Dave

My name is Dave Drobach, but most people know me as Replay Dave. I am 37-years-old. I currently live in Gainesville, Florida, and I have since 1995. I grew up in Deland, Florida, which is a small town about two hours or so away from here.

My parents are from up north. My dad got transferred to Daytona when he was working for General Electric, so from age zero to 17, I lived in the same house in Deland, Florida. I was born at Shand's Hospital because my mother was a diabetic. I remember being brought back to Shand's at an early age because they were trying to keep track of my development. I was probably 3 or 4—they had someone quizzing me on things—they would ask if a picture of something was correct or not. The one picture that I vividly remember was a woman with an umbrella, but the sun was out. I said, "That's not right, the sun is out!" Apparently that was the right answer and they were pleased; that was the first time I felt I knew something that I didn't know I knew, because no one had taught it to me.

I went to preschool in Deland at the Deland High School and it was pretty much just having fun—they would let us make crafts during the day. Then in kindergarten, I remember I would walk there as a 5-year-old so it wasn't that far from my house; I remember understanding the concept of zero and other basic math. After that, I went to St. Peters Elementary School, which is part of the Catholic church community that my family belonged to. It was a classic Catholic school that was taught by nuns and administered by nuns. I remember that the principal nun would come in and line students up—then she would drill them on multiplication tables. If you weren't fast enough she would yell at you.

I say this without a lot of bravado, but I exceled well in that environment, there was never an issue because I read well and learned math well (Figure 3.12). There are things that I learned at that school in 8th-grade science classes that I learned again at the University of Florida. The Catholic

Figure 3.12 Dave as a young boy.

educational system was a fantastic base of education for me. The warping of religion was also pumped into my brain—but I can't deny the good science and math there—even though you might not think there would be good science at a religious school.

As far as other learning, I remembered one of the first times I felt pain. My dad ran a tool cutting and grinding shop—it was an industrial setting. I would be there whenever my mom needed to run errands, so I would hang with my dad. When tools are sharpened and transported, they have to get coated in something so that the sharp edges don't run up against themselves and chip. It's like a hard half plastic oil material—basically that stuff sits in a crockpot all day and it gets heated to a very hot temperature. It becomes liquid so you can dip the sharp edge of the tool into it. At some point, this 350-degree oil and plastic mixture hit the top of my hand while I was dipping tools—I quickly learned that I had to get out of the way when it was dripping down the edge of the tool.

When I got older, I ended up working at that shop—I learned a whole bunch about cutting tools and how different materials react with other materials. That was the only time I ever used trigonometry in real life; using the knowledge of angles is very important when cutting tools. A tool that is cutting wood should be 15 or 20 degrees. When you are cutting metal like aluminum they should be like 7 degrees, or if you are cutting high speed steel, that should be 3 degrees. I learned all this from my dad.

I was also in the Boy Scouts of America as a youngster—I learned about knots, how to survive in the woods, what will hurt you, what won't hurt you. Being forced to be in close confines with other people, you learn to share, you learn to not be annoying—boys can be horrible to other boys and so when you see that, you think, "That's not nice, you should be nice"—so you get socialized. I had a fantastic experience with the Boy Scouts, I would recommend for any young man to go out into the woods with people that know what they are doing; all the things I learned are important things to know. My experience was something that I took for granted until later when I was out in a wood setting with other people—most people don't know how to have a relaxing experience in nature without all of their amenities.

Growing up in northern Florida, I learned what you do when you encounter an alligator in the wild—someone has to tell you that. They are really fast and they can eat you—they don't want to eat you—so you run in a zigzag or climb a tree. I haven't ever had a threatening face-to-face encounter with an alligator, but I have been around a few—and I know what to do. And also just basic things like how to remove a tick. Last week, we had a husband and a wife over, and there was a tick in her head from doing yard work earlier in the day. The husband was a little frazzled, so I stepped in, "I have this under control, don't worry about it, man." Thirty seconds later I had the full tick with the head with a pair of tweezers. The confidence of that comes from education. These are things that you learn—and not in a classroom.

My formal Catholic education ended after elementary school—the nearest Catholic high school would have been in Daytona Beach, and that wasn't in the cards financially. Deland High School was walking distance from my house and they had a great International Baccalaureate (IB) program there—it was a magnet school. I did get into the IB program, but I didn't understand how hard it was until I was a junior in high school and stopped the program. I wasn't really getting the grades and I didn't think that college was an option. I had the mentality of, "Why am I doing this? I have a car, I should just run around and listen to bands." The idea of reading about American history seemed boring. I guess that was when I became a poor learner.

Despite my grades, which were nothing to brag about, I did get accepted to the University of Florida for Summer B, which was the trial period that they give students that they accept conditionally. Summer B is for people they think will probably not cut it. So basically you showed up and if you could handle it, then you were accepted. Not only did I handle it, I got a 4.0.

For the most part at the University of Florida, I was an absolutely horrible student. It's not that I didn't get good grades; I just didn't crave the learning. I was passionate about anything *but* going to class and doing the work. Basically, I fell into the trap where I didn't really know what else to do with my life so I went to college, but then I branched out and started to do things I actually liked. When I was at Florida, I would walk from my dorm all the way downtown to see bands—I think it is hilarious to think of it now—I would always get there 2 hours before the band would play because I didn't want to miss a thing. I just wanted to be around it.

The summer between my junior and senior year in college, I went out traveling with a friend of mine and I learned quite a bit, not academically, but I learned my place, my class, and how other people perceived me. I learned how to navigate the world. We train hopped and took drive-away cars as far west as we could and made it back. We went to as many national parks and great sites that we could see. When you travel without money, you get creative and find ways to do things. Coming back from an adventure like that to sitting with 30 people in a classroom to just listen to people talk—it was maddening. At that point, I thought, "This is dumb, why am I here, what am I doing?" I did end up getting a degree in philosophy from the University of Florida—but I did toy with the idea of not finishing my degree, then I realized how foolish that would be in the grand scheme of things—I'm glad I did.

I first heard punk rock in my dad's machine shop. There was a guy a couple years older than me and he would play cassettes of cool music—Pennywise and Operation Ivy. That got me started on my quest for all things kick-ass. That guy would get other mix tapes and I would hear them; this was around the same time I had the feeling of wanting to express my own independence.

It's impossible for me to separate music that I think is good from music that is aggressive and antiestablishment. When I was growing up, I loved any idea that was anti-establishment. Ironically, the learning and the critical thinking that I got from my science classes in Catholic elementary school allowed me to see through all of the bullshit nuances of Christianity. I remember that there was a record store in Daytona Beach called Atlantic Sounds—it was there the first time that I saw the Bad Religion album *Suffer*—when I saw its cover, I lost it. The cover art is a cartoonish drawing of a boy living in suburbia—he is wearing a shirt with a cross with a "not" sign around it and he is engulfed in flames (Figure 3.13). I thought, "I need this—I am about this." The imagery was exactly how I was feeling—it was fantastic.

Figure 3.13 Bad Religion cover.

Punk rock began to shatter the veil that was cast on me as a child. I really connected with bands that conveyed ideas of destroying the veil of control through religion or control through government. I resonated with those bands, and they gave validation to the thoughts that I had about smashing the state or telling the Vatican to piss off...any of those ideas I was drawn to.

The band 7 Seconds, they really swung the pendulum for me. They took the angst and the frustration I felt when I listed to Pantera and they changed it. Pantera was just pure chaos and anger in a destructive manner, but 7 Seconds took that exact same thought pattern, feeling, logic and anger, but they turned it positive—turned it to building, instead of destroying. Or destroying in order to build. Being a 15-year-old male—my brain didn't make any sense to my body and my body didn't make any sense at all. 7 Seconds was able to guide that energy ball with the idea that, "You can do this, we can succeed where the hippies failed, we can build a better way, create our own culture, its okay." Anytime I would encounter something in literature or music that was destroying the bullshit fabric in a different way—I would gravitate towards it—relentlessly.

After that, I couldn't get music fast enough. When I like something, I want to know everything about it, everything associated with it. I would read the liner notes of the CDs and go find everything that was mentioned. I would see a band on a label and then I would go and find everything on that label.

Since I was 16, so in 20 years, there have only been a few months when I wasn't in an active band. There were enough punks in Deland to make up a few local bands, and the thing about Deland was that it was so small... I mean the culture of racism was not shy about itself, but it still happened sometimes that the 16-year-old Nazi skinhead guy would be playing bass with the antiracist Fishbone shirt wearing guy because there weren't that many of us. I want to be clear that I *never* played in a band with any racists, but there were times when it seemed like people were thinking, "I know you publically hate Black people and I publicly think that's stupid, but if we are going to cover this Minor Threat song, I need you." That was Deland, Florida, in 1992. We'd go to Orlando and see bands and the same people from the area would be there; I definitely did not move to Gainesville for the music culture, but once I got accepted to Florida, it was easy to find.

The most notable band I have been is Grabass Charlestons—who are now The Careeners. The most recent time I performed was two days ago. Our arc of success and popularity—I think that has been a slow curve. Each time we play, it gets better. Each time we record something, people know more about us. Touring was more about experiencing things—not that we believed that we had written the greatest songs ever. We wanted people to see us, but mostly we wanted to see things. If you have a goal, you don't need to have a booking agent. If your goal is just to get out and play, you don't need to have management or buses.

I started working at No Idea Records in 1996—just helping them assemble 'zine and CD packages. The need for me to work there grew from a once in a month thing to a twice a week thing. In 1999 I started working there full time and I have been there ever since. Right now I manage the production pieces of everything we do—and for a while I took over mail order when Matt, from Asshole Parade, went on tour. That was another way that I built relationships with punk organizers in their own towns.

Gainesville is a special place. The university brings a lot of new and excited freshness to town and it snowballs—everyone adds to it and there aren't that many people who are taking away from it. So me and all the other like-minded people who enjoy music and are nice to people did the work to build an infrastructure. Now, there are a plethora of places that take good care of touring bands and plenty of places for bands to practice where the cops won't shut them down. We have built all of that over the last 20 years. Once upon a time, my goal was to travel around the world until I found a better place to live, but I haven't found it.

Todd

Introduction

Before Todd and I met in person, he sent me a copy of his first book—the cover art is Todd lifting up his shirt to reveal a very large stomach tattoo: bright red and yellow flames surrounding the words BORN TO ROCK. Todd is of average height, boasts a shaved head, and wears black-rimmed glasses. Todd speaks with clear and firm intentionality—there is rarely any hesitation in his voice; he doesn't hold back any detail during the interviews and never reaches or strains to relay an answer. He speaks with a deep voice, but his tone is jovial and light-hearted—often laughing at himself while he speaks. An animated and energetic person, Todd has bold expressive eyes, as well as a keen sense of humor—often allowing for sarcasm or clever commentary to enter the conversation. He is also a humble narrator—often down playing his own successes and triumphs—there is no arrogance in his world.

During the interview, it is clear that Todd takes pride in living every aspect of his life according to his beliefs—where he lives, what he eats, how he travels, how he pays for things, and how he treats people are all manifestations of his ideals. He never sees an accomplishment as his to own alone—an authentic leader, he believes in modeling the behavior he wishes to see in those around him. Speaking to Todd and listening to him discuss the importance of punk, as well as his history of learning, means hearing stark and brutally honest responses. Not overflowing with emotion, Todd's stories revolve around straightforward facts as he saw them—surrounded by his opinions about them. Todd describes his life as being exactly how he wishes to construct it—as one that embodies DIY punk principles.

Punk Learner Profile

> *Inventors, I've always admired. By their very definition, they create something entirely new, something that had never existed before and could, quite possibly, change the world. How rad is that? Isn't that part of what punk's ideology is about? Changing the world. If even for a second. If even for a small group of people.*
>
> —Todd

My name is Todd Taylor and I am the editor and cofounder of the DIY punk 'zine *Razorcake*. I spent much of life in Boulder City, Nevada—but also lived my early childhood in Australia. I currently live in Highland Park, Los Angeles, and have lived here for 13 years. I have lived in California since 1995.

My mom was a stay-at-home mom and my dad was a social worker, and they were both of very modest financial means. My very first learning memories would have to be of my mom. She was a very, very hands-on mom and taught me a lot. I remember that she thought it was very important that she read to us—my brother and I—as children. We were living in Australia at the time, and we moved around a lot because of my father's job, so my mom was very good at adapting what we learned at school, or what we were taught at school so it would have a real world application. She was the one constant while we were moving so many places. I have such clear memories of my mother asking my brother how we could share a hamburger and each have the same amount of it; I remember her teaching me the idea of thirds. My parents were always reinforcing that we had to do house chores if we weren't studying; there was always a real big push for doing well in school.

I remember not being great at school, but just giving everything I could to it. I know I was a slow learner and I was a slow reader. It was difficult in Australia because we moved around so much that we were always dealing with different teachers, different classes, and different kids. Even though it was difficult, all the way through high school, my mother would not only make sure we were doing our work, but that we understood the work and that we could apply it to our lives. I think one of the underpinning skills she taught me was critical thinking and critical reasoning. So even if I didn't understand why I was learning it in school specifically, I still tried to get smarter because of it.

I'm a person who has often thought I knew something, but actually didn't. For example, I used to like to hang upside down in a tree as a child—and I knew that whenever you fell down from the tree, you hit the ground—you went down. So I figured, if you hung upside down, then I thought you would shoot into the sky (Figure 3.14). When I tried this, I hit my head really hard; that was the first of many concussions. I do a lot of failed learning that still happens to this day.

When I was in fourth grade, we moved to America—to Boulder City, Nevada. It's pretty isolated even though it's only 20 miles from Las Vegas. When I was growing up, there were 12,000 people, so it was pretty small. I think the whole high school was only 300 people. I think that during the time that I was in Boulder City, it was just very good standard schooling, nothing dazzling, but nothing harmful. I mean I went through high school pretty much unscathed and spent a lot of my time just doing my work and staying out of trouble. I just wanted to learn what I had to learn and then get out of there. I didn't want to talk to teachers too much about personal stuff.

Figure 3.14 Todd in a tree.

I tried to not take the easiest path through school; I tried to educate myself. I like being able to push myself mentally and know that it's possible to see what your limitations are and being okay with them. I was really an attentive student so if I had questions I would stay after and talk with the teachers... and I was fine with that. School exposed me to things I know I still love today: for example, I have an undying love of libraries because I spent so much time in the school and public libraries.

In high school, my SATs were not great, so I realized that I am not good at that type of testing. I fail in the sense that it doesn't give any credence to interpretive thought, to persistence, or reliability. Now, if you give me a question and I have to figure something out to get the answer, I can do it most of the time. If you give me a lot of stuff with abstract words that I never use and I'll never see again, I'm not going to do really well. I think I get kind of frustrated—it's almost a false education, like trivia. I don't like thinking that way and I never did well with standardized testing. I mean everything that I do on a day-to-day basis since I stopped formalized education has never had a process like that. If I don't know a word, I will look it up. If I want to know what context is, I'll study it. If I want to know about a specific person in a specific timeframe, I'll read them and try to figure it out.

Living in Boulder City was isolating, but there was a great radio station at the University of Las Vegas called KUNV, and at night it would play punk rock—that was my first time hearing it—and I would press record on my tape deck right before I would go to bed (Figure 3.15). Then there were some punk kids who transplanted from California—they were unlucky

Figure 3.15 Todd listening to KUNV.

bastards—to Boulder City and that's how I saw my first real punk rockers; and that's how it started. I taped the radio station onto a cassette, I would swap tapes with other kids, and then I found a couple of record stores in Las Vegas that had punk all the time. That led to finding shows through flyers—and the radio station was really good at announcing punk shows. I made friends that way.

When I was a young teenager, I was in a really bad car accident and a good friend died. My brother was in the car and he got injured, but I was in the hospital for a while. Before the accident, I was a really active kid—we rode bikes all the time, we'd go into the desert all the time, swim all the time. When I was recovering, I was debilitated for 8 or 9 months and I couldn't do anything active anymore. So I remember drawing at first and then writing stories just to write stories. I'd never done anything purely creative just to do it before. I'd always only done work if it was assigned to me. That was the first time where I thought in other ways. Creative writing and drawing were two big things that I lucidly remember starting to do. So I started writing and I listened to more punk rock—something that angry was awesome to me because my head was so out of whack.

Trying to locate punk music in Boulder City is like fun kid detective work. It was 1985 and there was an entire generation of disenfranchised punk rockers—people who didn't really care for it in the long run so I remember getting mix tapes, but they were totally mislabeled or not even labeled at all and then I spent years trying to figure out who was on the tape.

One thing I realized was that there were no firm edges to punk because I didn't know where the edge was. I would have music from 1977 England and from 1986 Las Vegas, but it would all be in the same context. There was very little history to it. The music I read about, I couldn't find personally and the music I found, I didn't have a lot of context for. I would go to the record store and talk to a guy named Louie the Letch, he taught me a lot.

After high school, I went to Northern Arizona University to go to undergrad and also finished my master's there too. It was fucking cheap and it was close. At the time, UNLV did not have an accredited English department. The other possibility was Reno, but Reno was 9 or 10 hours away and NAU was only 4 hours away. When I was living and going to school in Arizona, I'd go to a fair amount of punk rock shows, but Flagstaff, you know, there wasn't a lot going on. So during college, we would go down to Phoenix to go see shows. Not even small punk shows, but large shows of touring bands that we had heard of like Rocket from the Crypt or Helmet. In Flagstaff, there were people trying to put their bands together and bring other bands into town, so I saw the ALL/Descendents tour came through and Fugazi came through. So shows like that would happen, but it was once every 6 months or every 8 months.

Going through college, I put aside my personal feelings about college professors and the classes and just did it to the best of my ability to get out of there. I tried to learn beyond what was being presented. My parents just basically said, "Get your degree then you get a choice after that, if you get a job or you really fuck up you know you can still fall back on that." I internalized that too, I thought that was a pretty decent idea. It also gave me confidence to do other things beyond that and get completely out of that schooling system. I mean it's been almost 20 years now completely away from college and university.

When I graduated and I got my master's, I had a choice to go into a PhD program. I went and interviewed and I did fine, but I hated it. I knew what I *didn't want* to do more than I knew what I wanted to do a lot of times, educationally. Instead of going into a PhD program, I moved to California to live and spend time with my grandma. While I was there I dropped Flipside, a punk 'zine, a line and they finally got back to me. They asked, "Do you have a driver's license and will you really show up." I said yes to both. I worked in the morning roasting coffee, and then after I was done I would go out and help out at Flipside for three or four hours a day. When I was working at Flipside, I wanted to really throw myself into punk. Not only going to shows, but writing live reviews of those shows. Not only listening to some music, but hundreds and hundreds of records. I wanted to immerse myself, and educate myself, so I was intentionally trying to take in as much as possible. It was my self—I had access to a ton of great records that I'd only heard of. Flipside ended August 2000 and by that time I was basically running the entire operation with the exception that I didn't have any ownership of it. When Flipside ended, I thought this is the opportunity we have, I need to take it. It was a really painful time, but I thought that something really good could come out of it. Four months later, in January 2001, we started *Razorcake* to take over where Flipside ended. Our philosophy at *Razorcake* is to cover, support, foster, and celebrate the independent punk music community that lives below corporate media's radar.

Razorcake sifted through several different mottos before we decided on one (Figure 3.16). I wish I could say that I thought of the motto by myself, but it's actually from the WPA, the Work Project Administration, that funded a lot of the art projects during Roosevelt's New Deal. Their motto was "We Do Our Part." I really think it fits our mission because it is two things simultaneously. We do our part, meaning we spend all our time and energy putting *Razorcake* together—both the physical things and the concept of *Razorcake* together—because doing our part means that you have something physically tangible in your hand and it is a result of some physical, creative, or mental labor. On the other side of that is that we do *our* part—hopefully suggesting to other people for them to do *their* part. Like if we do not satisfy something that they want done, then they can do it for themselves as part of the DIY culture.

Figure 3.16 We do our part.

We also educate. For example, in one of our issues last year, we published our interview with Noam Chomsky. I want to focus on people that have a sustaining appeal because they are making meaningful music or doing meaningful things in politics. I mean, Noam Chomsky is not a flash in the pan; you may like him or you may not like him, but I want to document something that shows this man's contributions. A lot of punk rockers like to think they are anarchists, so let's inform them about what one really respected man's take on anarchism is.

I think quite a bit about the idea that the "medium is the message." What is being made is as important as what is being said—the noncorporate format of the 'zine is so important to me. I kind of liken it to the idea that *Razorcake* is a bunch of bricks—and the bricks represent our DIY punk community of people's work with us, but those bricks need to be formed into a bridge—we form that structure. Missing any of those people's hard work, we would be incomplete. We'd be a different thing... I don't think I would still be here if we didn't do this 'zine.

4

Punk and Education Horizons

> *Phenomenological text succeeds when it lets us see that which shines through, that which tends to hide itself.*
> —Max van Manen (1990)

> *There are always debates in punk rock. I think it was Kevin Dunn who said: If you put 15 punks in a room and ask them to define punk rock, you will get 18 definitions. I think that's a fair thing—and when I make that distinction, part of it is because punk rock is music and I don't want to be some one who imposes an ideology on music. I think a lot of people have done that with punk rock, but I want the music to just be the music. DIY has an ethos that has accompanied punk rock, but it isn't the only punk rock ethos, there isn't just one. There are 18 for every 15 punks.*
> —Sean Carswell (2011)

According to Eatough and Smith (2008), we make our lives by connecting the past with the present and future. This connection is a perceived one, as there are no exact concrete, linear paths to which all lives can subscribe. This making or meaning of our perceived life is not simple to capture by limiting our view to the superficial levels of our memories; therefore, using phenomenological interviews as a research method is an attempt to witness and record participants during a "making" of their life. Since there are countless memories, events, and emotions to share while you are considering the meaning of one's perceived life, it is helpful, and in some respects required, to use interpretive methods to present a few of many the possible meanings. These meanings are referred to as phenomenological horizons.

In Chapter 3, six researcher-constructed punk learner profiles were showcased as phenomenological narratives that addressed the research question: What is the experience of adults who conceptualize their engagement with punk as educative? In order to gain a cross-referenced understanding of the connective phenomena (Smith, Flowers, & Larkin, 2009; van Manen, 1990) among all six punk learners, it is illustrative to use interpretive phenomenological analysis (IPA) as a method of interpretation and analysis. As a way to gain a deeper sense of IPA and its service to phenomenology, it helps to have a brief reminder of the phenomenological research method, as well as an introduction to the IPA structure.

As discussed in-depth in Chapter 2, the qualitative research method of phenomenology aims to capture the essence of a specific lived experience. The focus of this is not on proving or concluding any sort of concrete finding, and the analysis should not carry any sense of judgment of the experience of the punk learner; rather, the intent is to bring to light what has been commonly unexplored in scholarship. Van Manen specifically promotes *embodied phenomenology*, that which uncovers the "life-world" we all live within, describes phenomenology as:

> The study of conscious experience...of individuals' perceptions, feelings, and lived experiences. It assists us in recapturing in ourselves the knowledge that life is bearable—not in the sense that we can bear it, as we burden which weighs us down, but in the sense that we know that life is there to bear us—as in the living in hope. (van Manen, 1990, p. 124)

Phenomenological Horizons

There are many ways to interpret phenomenological data or narrative; both narrative discourse (Genette, 1983) and literary comparison could also be appropriate philosophical matches with a phenomenological research base. According to van Manen (1990) and Smith, Flowers, and Larkin (2009), the essence of a shared experience (among several research participants) can best be discovered through a detailed interpretation using the categorization of themes or phenomenological horizons (see Husserl, 1913/1982). For this particular research, IPA is chosen to interpret the narratives of the six punk learners because it allows for a detailed and close reading of the accounts of lived experience, while also providing a clear protocol for cross-learner analysis. Additionally, IPA creates an interpretation that prioritizes the honoring of the punk learner's narrative, but doesn't neglect to address the need for transferability and relevant research to the discipline.

Interpretive phenomenological analysis (IPA) asks the researcher to access the meaning of an experience in an intimate enough way to uncover rich details, but without inserting themselves and their own judgments into the experience being accessed:

> Experience is itself tantalizing and elusive. In a sense, pure experience is never accessible; we witness it after the event. Therefore, when we speak of doing research which aims to get at experience, what we really mean is we are trying to do research which is "experience close." Indeed, because IPA has a model of the person as a sense-making creature, the meaning which is bestowed by the participant on experience, as it becomes an experience, can be said to represent the experience itself. (Smith, Flowers, & Larkin, 2009, 702–706)

The ways in which the learner makes meaning of an experience is, in short, representative of the experience and can serve as a way to expose the essence of a shared experience. In order to access the shared nature of an experience that has been part of more than one person's life, the IPA process is one that follows this cycle (Smith & Osborn, 2003):

1. Finding themes within transcriptions (close reading)
2. Clustering themes (phenomenological horizons)
3. Connecting themes with transcriptions (data coding)
4. Reflective writing (bracketing/reductio)

While using IPA, the researcher completes each part of the cycle and then repeats as necessary.

Table 4.1 provides a visual description of the horizons located within the phenomenological narratives of the six punk learners. Each horizon, as well as any subtheme of the horizons, is explored through transcription referral. In order to introduce language to the horizons present in the six narratives, the concepts of miseducative experiences (Dewey, 1938/1997) and educative healing (Olson, 2009) are used.

Punk As: Learner Self-Concept Awareness

For the purpose of this work, a learner self-concept definition pulls from Mercer's work and can be defined as, "the beliefs one has about oneself, one's self perception. It is not the 'facts' about oneself, but rather what one believes to be true about oneself" (Mercer, 2011, p. 14). The learner self-concept awareness horizon is of particular importance to this research as it sheds light on the ways in which the punk learners made sense of

TABLE 4.1 Phenomenological Horizons and Subthemes

What is the experience of adult punks who describe their engagement with punk as educative?

Horizon (Theme)	Sub-Theme	Participants (# of Punk Learners Who Identified With Horizon/# Total Participants)
Learner Self-Concept Awareness	Curiosity, Self-Direction, Confidence	5/6
	Apathy, Inadequacy, Resiliency	4/6
Miseducation	Hypocrisy/Betrayal	5/6
	Shame/Anger	3/6
	Disconnection	3/6
Education Healing	Empowerment and Inspiration	4/6
	Affirmation	4/6
	DIY Creation	6/6
	Ideals/Convictions	5/6
	Community	6/6

themselves as beings capable of engaging with the world as a learner. Putting words to and understanding their perceived identities as learners allows them to better describe and recall the ways in which punk engagement is educative. To conceptualize what is educative, one must have an idea of how, when, and most importantly who he/she is as he/she learns.

As each punk learner labors to describe their educative engagement with punk, the concept of a learner self-concept surfaced multiple times, as participants discussed memories of themselves at different developmental ages/periods in their lives. Each person identified as a learner in some manner either self-defined or was externally labeled by peers or schooling. Although each description was different and highly individualized, two groups of descriptors emerged as overlapping subthemes: curiosity, self-direction, and confidence; and apathy, inadequacy, and resilience. To a certain extent, each punk learner resonated with all six subthemes, but typically their narrative wording fell within these grouped constructs.

Curiosity–Self Direction–Confidence

The most commonly used descriptor of the learning self was that of a curious learner. When remarking on learning, Aaron describes himself as a "curious kid."

> I've always been naturally curious. So in middle school, which was the worst for so many reasons, I was still curious, the older I get the more curious I become.

Similarly, Erin describes her early life in elementary school as being informed by the curiosity and self-direction nurtured from her life growing up on a farm:

> I am a very curious person—I'm always trying to teach myself new things every day and trying to learn for myself. Being alone allowed me to figure things out for myself and entertain myself.

Todd describes himself as someone who sometimes "failed" at learning due to his curiosity:"I could tell you many times when I thought I had learned something... I always tried to learn beyond what was being presented." Sean describes his classes in elementary, middle, and high schools as places where he was bored, but also where he could "teach himself" while he waited for the teachers to instruct all of his other classmates. Sean continues to discuss all of the learning he undertook outside of school, where he confidently knew he could "figure things out" because he was "smart and capable":

> Most of my learning during those times was done outside of school. It kind of felt that if I wanted an education, then I had to do it myself. And, uh, a lot of my education K through 12 was me taking, taking it upon myself to educate myself about the things I was interested in.

Dave described his early learning self as adventurous and confident— he excelled in most learning contexts that he found himself in, whether in a school or out in nature, and described himself as a kid who "learned math and reading well," in addition to gaining critical thinking and inquiry skills during what he labeled a "fantastic education system." Dave also navigated nature well due to what he describes as "learning away from school"; whether it was knowing how to handle an alligator in the wild or removing a tick, Dave calls it the "confidence of that comes from education." He makes clear that education is "something that you learn," but not always in a classroom.

Todd, although he does not describe himself as an intuitively confident learner, identifies that his self-directed "hard work" allowed him to navigate learning sites well:

> I was really an attentive student. I tried to not take the easiest path through school, I tried to educate myself. If I don't know a word, I will look it up. If I want to know what context is, I'll study it. If I want to know about a specific person in a specific timeframe, I'll read them and try to figure it out.

Distance–Inadequacy–Resilience

Not all participants could easily describe their learner self-concept, Yam attempted to put language to the ways he felt toward himself as a learner, even though he had spent his entire life in some sort of schooling. He described himself as an "apathetic" learner who felt "distant" and "disengaged" with learning sites during his adolescence. This attitude carried into his high school life, and in terms of his college goals, he recalls feeling as if "nothing seemed like a good option." Similarly, both Todd and Sean described themselves as "distant" from their peers and teachers in school. Sean recalls his earliest memories in elementary school:

> I remember this feeling a lot in school—this feeling that I would try to learn things on my own first, and then I would just sit in class and be bored. When I was bored, I did a lot of writing: short stories, fiction. But I remember feeling disconnected from the rest of my class.

Other times, the learner self-concept was marked as inadequate by a schooling process. Todd described himself as "slow learner" with "limited capacity," saying, "I'm not naturally gifted at learning, I'm just not a talented guy that way." He goes on to describe himself as "not being great at school" because he was a "slow reader in first and second grades." Similarly, Aaron describes feeling like an "outsider" in school where he was "made to feel stupid" by his peers and teachers. Erin describes her learner self-concept in the upper grades in school as "bad" and a "stubborn and indignant learner."

At times, learner resilience was characterized as part of the learner self-concept, primarily to survive or "get through" school. Todd describes his learner resilience as "robotic"; when something would be assigned to him, he would get all of his work done quickly so he "wouldn't have to think about schoolwork." Erin described her learner resilience through the "getting by just enough to pass" the classes that were difficult for her: "I got a D in math every year so I wouldn't have to take it senior year. If I passed enough math, I could opt out of it."

Dave recognized that although he wasn't a passionate learner in college, he managed to continue forth so that he could "finish and start to do things" he was really interested in: "I was an absolutely horrible student; not that I didn't get good grades, but I didn't crave the learning."

Yam described his resilience as thinking of school "like it was a job" and focusing on what life would bring him when he was "finally done with school":

I felt like "I have to get done with school." And it was always possible enough to get decent grades, enough to get by, So it was mainly just thought about, like, how someone would go to a job, I just gotta do this.

Punk As: Miseducative Experience Awareness

For the purpose of this research, the term "miseducation" is used specifically as John Dewey, education philosopher and scholar of the early-20th century, in his work *Experience and Education*, defines it:

> The belief that all genuine education comes about through experience does not mean that all experiences are genuinely or equally educative. Experience and education cannot be directly equated to each other. For some experiences are miseducative. Any experience is miseducative that has the effect of arresting or distorting the growth of further education. An experience may be such as to engender callousness; it may produce lack of sensitivity and of responsiveness. (Dewey, 1938/1997, p. 26)

For an experience to be miseducative, Dewey remarked that it would have to halt the intuitive or natural growth of further education. Additionally, the learner's experience would promote negative feelings toward learning in general, the content, or him or herself as a learner; such feelings could be "callousness," as Dewey describes, but also resentment, shame, defeat, anger, or bitterness. In other words, learners can have the "wrong kinds of experiences" that create a dissonance to both the concept and act of learning; where the learner loses "the impetus to learn because of the way learning was experienced by them" (p. 26).

With this in in mind, if we are to use Dewey's language to interpret the punk learners' narratives, the mentions of "miseducative" experiences are vast and plentiful. Each punk learner shared, at length, experiences that caused negative feelings about learning, about academic content, and about themselves as learners. These miseducative experiences are especially important to note here in this research due to the need for the punk learners to articulate that which further explicates how and when they learn. In order to unpack how punk has been educative, the punk learners' sought to explore what has hindered or stunted their education growth as well. Given that phenomenological research's goal is to present an experience through the ways in which the person perceives the experience, I have categorized the miseducative experiences based on the primary emotive descriptions of hypocrisy and betrayal, anger and shame, and disconnection.

Hypocrisy and Betrayal

The instances of miseducative experiences that were triggered by a sense of betrayal or hypocrisy were many, with all six punk learners referencing a spectrum of impact on their lives. In the following vignettes, the punk learners reveal experiences where the primary feeling was of betrayal from a system they trusted, largely resulting from an increased awareness of hypocritical behavior.

Todd spent much of his boyhood in Boulder City, Utah. Self-described as an "active kid" who loved riding bikes and being outdoors with the Boy Scouts, his most "impactful" miseducative experience occurred when he was 15-years-old:

> My brother and I were counselors in training at a Boy Scout camp. We were there for an extended period of time and when we were being driven back by our friend, the tire blew out and the car flipped over several times. I was ejected through the front windshield. Pat, my friend who was driving, actually made the initial hole in the windshield. If he hadn't, I probably would have been dead, too. Pat died on impact.

> The Boy Scouts wanted nothing to do with us—their advice to us was to sue Pat's family... which we weren't going to do. The organization that is supposed to protect you—you buy into the organization and at a time of need, we were saying, "Hey we need help here—something bad happened and it's on your watch," they completely divorced themselves from it. That left a really big impression on me to this day. I have a hard time with larger power structures that aren't answerable—if they ask a lot of you as a citizen, or whatever, as a member of that community, it should be answerable to you in some way shape or form. That was very, very, impactful.

Similarly, Dave's miseducative experiences stem from his community ties. Although Dave's experience in religious elementary school was largely positive, describing it as "fantastic," he also acknowledges knowing, "the warping of religion was also pumped into my brain." It wasn't until eighth grade that Dave significantly questioned what he had been taught to believe about Catholicism and his country:

> The exact spark was watching the Geraldo Rivera special about satanism, it was 1991 and he was detailing these horrible satanic rituals. People were freaked out about it—he had this line about human sacrifice and blood drinking, and my brain says, "Huh, that sounds exactly like a Catholic mass. Why is one thing okay, and one thing horrible? You are teaching me that in the Catholic mass, that it's actually the flesh and blood of Jesus Christ, everyone lines up to consume it—that is Holy—and you need to do that to get the heaven prize. Yet someone else does that for another deity, and it is the most horrible, unspeakable, put-them-in-prison type thing."

My brain started connecting and seeing things as hypocritical. There was hypocrisy taking place in government! We are told, "Yeah everyone is equal" except these people, and these people, and this gender they aren't equal, but "everyone is equal" [noting sarcasm] and "America is the greatest place in the world," except we do all these horrible things.

A few punk learners mentioned miseducation examples specific to their disappointment in an educational system that did not give them the support they needed in specific academic content; both Aaron and Erin mention troubles with math in particular. Aaron attributes his challenges with understanding math to his early education in his private Baptist school:

> I have always struggled with math my whole life, I still do. So there was definitely attention that I needed as a young kid that I didn't get.

Erin, who attributes her struggles with math to her participation in her gifted program, recalls an early memory:

> At my elementary school, the gifted program was always taught by the art teacher. So when you got taken out of your regular class, you always went to the art room. They would always pull me out of math, and I'm still horrible at math.

Similarly, Sean also found his miseducative experiences within the ways that testing "wasted his time" because it wasn't an "authentic" demonstration of his learning:

> A lot of school in the 70s, and Florida in the 80s, too, was very much about standardized testing. Standardized testing is based on a formula, and I could probably pass multiple-choice tests even if I knew nothing about a subject because they follow a pattern. There's two possible answers, two ridiculous ones, and you just guess between the two and you'd probably do okay. I mean it was just such a fucking waste of time. When in life do you ever do a multiple-choice test? Even for a 9-year-old, I think I could just see that it was a waste of my time. Sitting down, shutting up and picking A through D was useless to me.
>
> And even as big of a reader as I was, to do those reading comprehension tests where they picked the most boring articles, and then they just see if you can find a word in there and define it in context. To me reading comprehension seemed like, "How well can you stay awake through this incredibly boring article and then say four obvious things about it?" I mean I just hated that—I hated that stuff.

Todd continues to talk about the ways testing did not authentically measure his understanding or love for literature, even well into graduate school:

You didn't have to have a real knowledge or a greater understanding of how to make an awesome paragraph, or how to make a paragraph that has both a lot of information, but is also available to a wide audience. Those things were important to me, but with tests, these things almost seemed like games. When I got my MA in literature, I felt like I had a pretty good grasp on certain things in literature, but I remember the GREs being a game too. I mean I can't tell you who Samuel Johnson was in a fight with many of hundreds of years ago, and it just seemed to me like a parlor trick.

If I don't care about it, it's hard for me to really engage with it. Tests are very difficult for me, they make me very anxious and I'm not good at them.

Shame and Anger

Aaron's miseducative experiences with schooling began at a very early age when he recalls the shame he felt in his Baptist elementary school:

> Thinking back on that school, there was all kinds of real bad negative shit that happened to me when I was there. I wasn't sexually abused or physically abused, but I was physically paddled in front of my peers, made to bend over the desk and paddled with a board in front of all my classmates—really humiliating stuff. I remember singing that song from Flashdance, "She's a maniac, maniac!" I was singing that and I got paddled for that. It was fire and brimstone Christianity. I remember being in the pastor's office and him getting close to my face and telling me that I was weak and that God was angry with me and that God hates a weakling. "Look at you crying" and you know, I'm in the third grade, and this big towering red-faced man, reeking of Old Spice and sweat, was in my face and telling me that I'm weak, and God is angry at me, and then scaring the shit out of me, and then paddling me. My mom still feels guilty about it to this day. When she hears me talk about it, you can tell she feels embarrassed, because she knows that I am a devout athiest now.

Aaron's miseducative experiences didn't end with the physical abuse, but rather continued emotionally and academically as he was moved from Baptist schooling to a public school in fourth grade:

> When it came time to actually do schoolwork, I didn't know how to multiply numbers, I didn't really know how to tell time on a clock, and that's when I realized that I had been cheated, so I was angry. Because when you are that age, you don't want to feel like an outsider—you don't want to feel stupid. And I remember being made to feel that way because the kids made fun of me.

> At the Christian school, everybody's parents came to the carpool to pick everybody up—there weren't school buses. And I remember walking out the front doors of public school and panicking because I didn't know how I was gonna get home, because I didn't know what bus to get on—and everybody was making fun of me. It was pretty traumatic, you know? So my history as a learner was pretty stilted because of that time—because of my early education.

Erin discusses her struggles with math into middle and high school, she uses algebra as the first academic example of her feeling "ashamed" at not understanding content in school:

> I think, growing up and everybody in elementary school telling you how smart you are all the time, how special you are, but wait, "You are not really good at algebra—you need help with this." But I didn't know how to ask for help; I had not had to before. So I would just be failing horribly and my parents would never know—I would never tell anyone that I was doing badly. Because I thought I would get in trouble, it made me feel bad about myself. So I would dig myself into holes that I couldn't get out of, because I would get so far behind in my work. I would fail so many tests and I would throw them away or hide them. Looking back, I could have just been like, "I need a tutor," but it made me feel ashamed to not do well at things.

Aaron's feelings of being an "outsider" continued as he moved from West Virginia to Florida. He described it as being "moved from a foreign environment to another foreign environment," where he "immediately stuck out, got beat up, got picked on—the teachers were checked out." In high school, Aaron's notices all of his friends from middle school have dropped out:

> So then it was just me with all the same jocks and all the same rednecks, but there was only one of me, and I got shit all the time from all the other people in my school.

Additionally, many of Aaron's miseducative experiences stemmed from his interactions with specific teachers. He recalls feeling like "the teachers were against us, it was so alienating and the teachers were shitty. I remember the first time I smelled gin, I was like, "Oh, that's Mr. Franklin, that's why he was so awful—he was fucking drunk on gin all the time!" One of the more vivid experiences is during his eleventh grade English class:

> I remember that we were reading Macbeth and I was really into it.... In the middle of the reading, the teacher interrupted the reading and said, "Aaron, look at your pants!" My jeans were frayed at the bottom, which was against dress code, so she kicked me out of class and told me to go to the principals office. I'll never forget that, and I was like, "Wait, you are kicking me out of class? Because of my pants? You are taking me away from learning?" Her name was Ms. Jenota and I made her cry because I told her she should be ashamed of herself for pulling me out of class, taking me away from learning even though I'm not bothering anyone. I was like, "You've got guys outside fucking selling weed in the parking lot, and you've got people fighting in the gym, and you are kicking me out of class for my pants? Fuck you!" And so high school was terrible.

Like Aaron, Erin's miseducative experiences were also connected with her poor inter-relationships with teachers. Although she describes herself as a "hard worker" and curious learner in her early schooling, she steadily "gave up" on learning because of the ways in which her interactions with teachers led her to believe that she could not succeed as a learner:

> I think it was the personalities of teachers that I had to deal with. Teachers who I thought were hard asses and that I didn't think that I was learning anything from, I completely shut down with them. The teachers would just berate me. One was my 9th-grade Spanish teacher who told me that I wasn't even good enough to go to college. I had an environmental science teacher that would tell me that every time I came to class, he knew how much I didn't care.
>
> Another memory I have was with a really strict chemistry teacher. I had messed up some homework and I was trying to talk to her about it. She was like, "I know you are just a liar." She had heard I was a liar from my 10th-grade teachers; they told her about me being a bad kid. She was like, "I know that you are bad." I thought, "Shit, man, this is every class I go to."
>
> So I just stopped going. I was just like, "Well, fuck it. I don't want to go to school anymore." So I would skip school all of the time. I wasn't used to doing bad at school—I had always done really well. So I think it was just that I got behind, I got frustrated, I got angry, and then I just didn't go anymore. Seems like a natural progression of just giving up.

Erin proceeds to discuss how these interactions with teachers impacted her ideas about who she was as a learner:

> I don't think I started bad. I think I'm pretty stubborn—I think I'm probably pretty indignant, but its not hard to convince me to work hard for something. But it was just easier for me to be bad, to stop going to school. I don't know. It chips away at your confidence when people think you are bad; it makes you believe you don't deserve to try harder or to want something. So you become bad.

Todd remarks that he "graduated from high school pretty much unscathed." Yet he also states that he was a "slow reader" and that standardized tests and reading comprehension exams were problematic for him, since they did not do justice to represent what he knew or his skills:

> I've always felt slow. Like I feel a lot slower than other people. When I'm given a lot of information, it takes me a long time to percolate through it. If you give me a bunch of stuff, I can't just shoot it right back at you. My SATs were not great, I am not good at that type of testing. I fail in the sense that it doesn't give any credence to interpretive thought, to persistence, and also, like, reliability. If you give me a question and I have to figure something out

to get the answer, I can do it most of the time. If you give me a lot of stuff with abstract words that I never use and I'll never see again, I'm not gonna do really well. I think I get kind of frustrated. SATs struck me as almost like a false education, like trivia, like you figure out the puzzle, but not inside the puzzle. When looking at the questions, I'm deducting that I have a high possibility that it's B or C, but I don't know—I don't like thinking that way. I never did well with standardized testing.

Disconnection

Yam was clearly dissatisfied with his schooling experiences, and could isolate his miseducative experiences to the ways in which he "had no voice" in any classroom, which left him feeling "disengaged," and with a general distaste for the teachers and the peers he went to school with. Yam describes his feelings as a "reaction to the busywork of public school":

> I just felt like there was just so much busywork that was constantly being put upon you to complete, and that there's just no reason to do it other than to keep you in the classroom. I've forgotten everything other than like basic math and maybe like some geometry. I question if any of it is really worth it. But I did it just to get it over with so I could do my own stuff. The goal was to be done with school forever.

Sean's experience in schooling left him feeling "bored" and "disconnected":

> I remember my elementary education—being disconnected from the rest of my class. You know I wasn't the only one; there were other smart kids in the class, we were all disconnected. It was kind of one of these educational systems where they teach to the lowest performing kid in the class, and if you're not low performing then what do you do in class? You just kind of sit there. Which is, I think, maybe what schools are supposed to predominantly teach kids—to sit down and shut up. Get here on time, sit down and shut up. Especially in working-class schools, they have that factory mindset in the 70s. So that was elementary school. And that was junior high. And then, in all honesty, that was high school.

Aaron's experiences were on more of a personal community scale as he describes his feelings about the rural town he grew up in:

> College—it seemed like it would never happen—it was definitely not a sure thing at that point. I had no plan, you know. And a lot of that goes back to when my dad got hurt when I was five. I realized at a young age that shit happens like that, so I thought that there was no need to make long-term plans or have long-term goals because I could be dead in 5 minutes. And I remember thinking, at like 5 or 6, "Wait, my dad just went to work and now he is never gonna walk again." That definitely shaped my actions.

108 ■ *DIY Punk As Education*

Punk As: Educative Healing

> *When I'm an old, old, man, I will always know that the sweetest and greatest things that I have in my life and gotten to experience in my life, have been directly or indirectly linked to my interest in punk rock. For sure, without question.*
> —Aaron

In her book, *Wounded By School,* Kirsten Olson (2009) describes the specific ways in which schooling can and does wound learners. Olson chronicles the stories of a varied group of people and categorizes their school wounds in order to shed light on the manner in which schooling can be more detrimental to a student's psyche than the accepted narrative of "hard" or "challenging." In her final few chapters, Olson also details the ways in which her interviewees discussed the ways in which they attempted to heal their wounds. Although Olson's research is restricted to wounds and healing related to primary schooling, her concepts of education healing can be expanded to be helpful in the process of unpacking and interpreting the narrative data associated with the participants' educative healing experiences in punk.

In Olson's work, she draws connections between students' experiences and attitudes, and their education healing; themes of peer and community support (pp. 97–98), affirmation of identity and experience with success (pp. 93–94), and awareness of strengths (pp. 99–100) were tagged as "commonalities of healing" (p. 87). Using Olson's frame as inspiration, I interpreted the narrative data to reveal the following educative healing horizons: do-it-yourself (DIY) creation, empowerment and inspiration; affirmation, ideals, and convictions; and community.

Empowerment and Inspiration

> *At the core of it, take some initiative in your life and how you are living it. Don't accept the culture that is given to you, make your culture.*
> —Sean

During the interviews, there were consistent descriptive narratives detailing feelings of empowerment and inspiration that stemmed from punk engagement. The role of an empowered learner in an educative context is an important one for exploration, particularly when identified within what is typically referred to as an out-of-school context or informal site of learning.

Aaron, a self-described "angry" learner who had felt "cheated" by his early education experience, described the merging of his punk engagement with his empowered self-directed learning:

> It was tenth grade when I started taking charge of my own learning. I started being very interested in punk rock and literature, both things worked in tandem and made me think: "School is bullshit, but that doesn't mean I have to give up." I remember walking around after I was deeply, deeply into punk rock and started reading Kurt Vonnegut and Jack Kerouac. I remember walking down the hall in high school with a better feeling: I felt like, "You know, you guys are all fucking idiots and you guys are all assholes, but I know shit you don't and fuck you." And I remember that it was comforting. I didn't feel as tragic about it anymore. I felt empowered.

Yam, who had largely been apathetic toward engagement with formal learning, became empowered and "inspired" by punk:

> I'm always working, always having a band, always working on a 'zine—struggling to set up shows any way I could. It was at this time [after high school] that I started to do stuff... because all of a sudden I felt that I could do stuff.

Similarly, Erin, who often struggled to find comfort in her own skin as a student or artist, found additional comfort, inspiration and empowerment through her engagement with her punk community:

> I can be involved in community things that I want to be involved in. My friends are all doing things that I am excited about. I can be a helpful part of that. Whereas before, I didn't know where I fit in with anything at school. I thought, "I don't really know what I'm doing here." But when I am with my community here doing stuff, it makes sense to me and its empowering.

Sean interprets his efforts, both at *Razorcake* and through his faculty position, as an educational effort to empower the ideas of those engaged in the punk community.

> The idea is that something gets triggered, and you read something in Razorcake, and then you have a conversation with someone about it. We are independent of it, but we are still a part of it. It's better than someone saying something and then someone else saying something back, but no one is actually listening. Instead now, everyone is listening and people have ideas and we spread it out. I learned from punk that you should have some intention to what you are doing. And you can take that into your schooling and I think people should. I try to offer this as a suggestion to my students: You can study intentionally and deliberately.

Affirmation

> *Living in a community such as mine leaves you a lot more room to be alternative or broken or different.*
>
> —Erin

As mentioned in Chapter 2, much of the academic discourse on punk acknowledges identity construction as a major component of engagement. Similarly, the six punk learners differentiated the affirmation that was felt from their punk community, and juxtaposed it with their other feelings of alienation and disconnection. For many participants, punk was one of few sites of learning that validated their existence and where they felt seen. This affirmation not only prompted the punk learner's initial interest in punk, but also kept them engaged throughout their adult lives.

As one of the few punk learners that didn't describe his schooling as "traumatic," Todd described himself as a "good student." He "kept his head down, completed his work, and stayed out of trouble," yet he was also a "distant" learner who didn't build relationships with teachers. After his car accident and the betrayal he felt as a result of his experience with the Boy Scouts, he looked for a place to go in order to process his anger:

> That's the thing about the accident I had was that's when I first started listening to punk rock because something that angry was awesome because my head was so out of whack.

Dave found affirmation during an especially transitory time in his life when he was seeking additional perspectives on what he interpreted as religion and governmental hypocrisy. Like many who are engaged with punk, lyrics, records, and album artwork provide anchors for this type of exploration. Dave recalls the very first specific instance where his search for meaning was affirmed:

> I remember that there was a record store in Daytona Beach called Atlantic Sounds. It was there the first time that I saw the Bad Religion album "Suffer." When I saw its cover, I lost it. The cover art is a cartoonish drawing of a boy living in suburbia; he is wearing a shirt with a cross [crucifix] with a "not" sign around it and he is engulfed in flames. I thought, "I need this, I am about this." The imagery was exactly how I was feeling—it was fantastic.

Similarly, Yam found affirmation in punk lyrics and community while he was looking to find his place in the social justice minded aspect of punk. His affirmation triggered a desire to engage with political punk, but on his own terms:

I feel like, the approach was, it was okay to be yourself. Like the revolutionary aspect of what is in political punk was like, "If you're not part of the revolution, like, not in the revolution right now, then you are not doing your part." And that created a very real delusion of what being political meant. With Dillinger Four, it was all, like, "We are all just doing this, we are all doing what we can and we all gotta get by somehow." And it was just much more real to me than the other bands I had experienced at the time.

Aaron describes a vivid memory of attending punk shows in Gainesville as a teenager before he became a musician; he was fascinated with the ways in which he was seen and affirmed by people he respected and looked up to:

I started coming to Gainesville and going to record stores where I could buy a 7-inch for two bucks. And going to shows where people would give me 7s. It was so exciting; all of that was so exciting to my teenage brain. I thought that was so cool—I mean I'm holding this 7-inch record, and the band just got the money together and they made this fucking record. They recorded it, they sent it off, and had this record made. They screen-printed their own covers and they gave me one! I thought that was so cool. It was immediately interesting and immediately exciting. It was affirming.

Like Aaron, affirmation also presented itself to Dave in the form of peers:

Seeing bands play in a small setting without bouncers and ticket stubs and all that was a big step of being treated as a peer. I remember vividly, walking around campus as a 17-year-old, with baggy shorts and a chain wallet and a Bad Religion T-shirt and having people hand me flyers for punk shows. It felt like a gesture of acceptance—it was great—an acceptance, and it was closer to that peer relationship.

Do-It-Yourself (DIY) Punk Creation

The essence of punk is equality, open self-expression, and to help people express themselves... it can be so many different things and also be nothing at the same time. That's why I'm much more interested in being productive and working to create something.
—Yam

My first impression of people is what can we do together? What can we make together?
—Todd

Mageary (2012) describes do-it-yourself (DIY) as an,

ethical and practical stance [that] now pervades punk culture, from booking shows to writing and recording music to the production of clothing, 'zines, and other cultural artifacts. It is such an integral element of punk that many participants cannot separate the two. (p. 63)

This DIY creative element was referenced consistently throughout all of the interviews, and is particularly relevant to a discussion on education healing, since the concept of independent, empowered creation is an important aspect of advanced self-directed learning. The mention of DIY creation was largely referencing two areas: artistic contribution to punk culture (i.e., 'zines, music, shows) and academic endeavors. Aaron discusses the artistic messaging of DIY in punk music:

> I've always been interested in music and art, but this one kind of music moved me. I loved the sound and the aggression, I loved trying to figure it out; there was something about punk rock that seemed personable and approachable. Hearing the Dead Milkmen for the first time, it was just DIY—people doing what they wanted, because that's what they wanted to do. Anyone can do it! I mean those bands are telling you to do it. The Minutemen are telling you to go start your own band. You should create, you can also be a part of this. You don't get that same message when you listen to a Slayer record. It's a separate thing; it's like watching a movie, you aren't part of it. Listening to the Minutemen, you are being told that you should be a part of it.

Similarly, Sean describes his creative inspiration from his punk engagement as a clear understanding that

> with punk rock there is an ethos of DIY right from the beginning. If you don't like the way music is, start your own band. If you don't like the way music is recorded or packaged, then start your own music label. If you don't like the way distributors handle things, then start your own distro. If you don't like stores, make your own store. So book your own tours, set up your own venue. All of those things.

Yam, who had originally described himself as a "disengaged" and "disconnected" learner, whose sole goal in life was to be "done with school forever," discusses the way in which he evolved into "creating" for himself for the first time after high school:

> So, all the way up to ninth grade, I was incredibly inactive compared to how much I was talking about punk music—just like a lot of talking about what it meant to be punk—but never actually following through with any of it. But when I graduated high school, I began setting up shows and doing 'zines and being in a band, whereas all through high school it would just be talking about that stuff. I just had a breaking point one day, just like "We're doing it!" I remember walking down the street and walking past a place that had shows and walking in and asking can I set up a show here and them being like, "Uhhh, sure." That was the first show I set up.

For Aaron, his awareness of DIY also manifested as an academic realization, where punk was a "very significant breath of fresh air... where the world just kind of cracked wide open." He saw the DIY ethic as something that could immediately pertain to his engagement with literature, a content area that he loved:

> Vocabulary, now I definitely remember this... I definitely remember looking up words, like, "What does that mean?" I remember writing down words and thinking, "I guess I'm spelling it right" and I'd look up words I didn't know. Pixies are the first band that came to mind. I remember listening to the Pixies and looking up unfamiliar vocabulary—you know, that's when I was learning.

Like Aaron, Sean's drive to independently create had a significant impact on his learner identity, but it was primarily during his formal post-secondary education. He "tried to be autonomous" in his graduate school education, so he recalls an experience with his very first semester with a professor that he felt was disengaged:

> When I realized what this class was gonna be and when I realized I had moved across country to be in this class, I thought I gotta fix this and I gotta find some people that are gonna make this experience worthwhile. There was some punk rockers in the class and I thought, "all right, I know this community—DIY—and these guys are DIY guys and I can go work with them, and we can build our own shit, and we'll do it ourselves, if were not happy." You know, the whole idea behind punk rock, if your not happy with the media, become the media. And so by extension, if you don't like the way this class is going, if you're not getting enough out of it, start your own class out of it. And so I went and teamed up with those guys, and so we taught each other. The whole DIY aspect of punk really took over my master's education at that level.

The DIY punk ethos is often attached to the production and distribution of music, as well as the logistics of touring bands. In this manner, as a musician, Dave's understanding and experience with DIY creativity was connected to his role in a band:

> You can't be a jerk. If you aren't a jerk, you can do anything in the DIY world. A lot of people that I consider close friends and I, we can see a way around anything. You just need to see it in a different capacity. You don't need to have a booking agent, and you don't need to have management or buses if your goal is to just get out and play someplace. If you have an idea of an end result, you can do that or you can the frills. If you know the goal and see it and visualized it, then you go.

The DIY ethic did not only pertain to individual wants and desires around creation, but was also manifested a spirit to aid punk community efforts beyond playing an instrument in a band. Yam describes the importance of the DIY ethos in the maintenance of punk 'zines and organizations:

> DIY punk is getting stuff done, not as fast always, but just getting stuff done no matter what it takes and being as resourceful as possible. Being here [at Razorcake] has expanded my ideas of... not like punk business, but how punk can exist in business models. Like how things can operate and still be punk. It doesn't have to be chaos all the time.

In a similar way to Yam, Erin saw her role as one that fed and pushed the DIY punk community forward through means that were not directly related to playing music or setting up shows. For Erin, DIY punk engagement meant that she could become a "legitimate artist" within the punk community, which meant

> being able to execute what you see mentally in a way that is your own, and then you get good enough at it that other people think you may be able to represent an aspect of their own craft that they might need and can't execute themselves. Through making fliers and album art, I was able to be involved in the music scene that I so valued, despite not playing an instrument. Lyrically, all of these bands have comforted me, brought me back to life and given me visuals through lyrics when I was stuck. It also makes me feel strong and able. To be recognized for what you love doing is really a confidence booster most of the time. I think it tires me out, but it doesn't emotionally zap me like being involved in things that don't feed me back, like jobs or school or negative relationships.

Ideals and Convictions

> *Everything that I've done, everything that I champion, is linked to punk. There is no way it can be understated.*
> —Aaron

> *You can talk about this stuff as much as you want, but if you aren't living it in a way that really affects your livelihood, that investment is not really there.*
> —Todd

> *I took punk rock ideology as being deliberate—most people aren't deliberate—and that's what punk rock teaches you, do shit on purpose.*
> —Sean

Much has been written about the intuitive nature of political activism and liberal ideology associated with punk (see Andersen, 2004; Kuhn, 2010; Marcus, 2010), therefore it was of little surprise that the interviewed punk learners identified exposure and adoption of punk ideals and convictions as a significant piece of their educative engagement in punk. Although highly connected to their own individual stories, the ideals and convictions discussed during the interviews broadly fell into two areas: personal and political.

Erin describes the early "shaping" of her punk values through the feminist punk movement RiotGrrl, because "it embodied music, performance, art, zines, and activism."

Yam was struck by the difference between the pop punk that was being played on the radio in the 1990s and the "real punk" that was rooted in political activism:

> There are real politics in punk music, and so I probably went over board with that... like, saying, "No this is real punk! Political punk! Like communism... this isn't pop music." My band is Dillinger Four. I had a vague recommendation, so I picked up that CD and read the lyrics and that kind of broke walls down for me. I knew punk was political, but now I knew it wasn't only raising your fist and waving a flag, but it was also thinking, "I'm not going to give in"... And like being true to yourself in a real way and not a slogan way; so like that was a massive wall that came down. That was the first time I listened to music where I felt it had conviction, but it wasn't trying to posture about it. Whether those be political convictions or personal convictions—and they blurred that line between personal and political conviction, too—made it all seem important and all very urgent, and that was the first time I had read lyrics like that.

Aaron discussed the beginnings of his understanding the political convictions of punk, which led him to make connections between song lyrics and other sources of information, and which assisted him in unpacking political and social contexts:

> I mean, most of the time, I didn't understand what I was hearing... and I didn't understand most of the politics, but I caught on along the way. You know you are just starting to question things about the world and be somewhat aware about politics. And I'm seeing all these things pop up in the music I'm listening to; and that was one of the things I loved about punk rock—it could be totally ridiculous, funny and in jest, you know. Like there are songs about doing laundry and then there are songs about Cambodia, like, "Where is Cambodia? What the fuck is going on in Cambodia?" I mean this is before the Internet, so it's funny to think of things in that context. I would hear something, or I would read something, and I would think, "Oh, that's the reference"—like Jerry Brown or Nixon or Cambodia or Reagan especially. Or I would read things and think, "Oh, post-WWII prosperity"... So just little tidbits would help me make connection along the way. Little pieces of the puzzle, "Oh, this is why the suburbs exist to a certain extent," and "This is why the Descendents are bummed out about the suburban home."

Like Aaron, Dave's convictions grew more intense and affirmed as he further engaged with punk:

> When I was growing up, I came from the school of Jane's Addiction—I thought, "That's not the stuff I learned about in my religious upbringing!" Connecting with bands that also had the same idea of destroying that veil or controlling through religion or controlling through government, resonated and gave validation to the thought that I had about smashing the state or telling the Vatican to piss off. Any of those ideas I was drawn to.

Although not necessarily viewed through a political activism lens, Yam describes how his work has led him to have a greater understanding of what he calls "punk pedagogy" with his work within organizations, whether it is his band or his community:

> One of the main ideas behind punk is that it should be accessible, and two, it should be affordable, which I guess is another form of accessibility. And so I'm constantly thinking about ways to minimize costs for ourselves so we can pass that on to people who might want to purchase stuff, and also constantly looking for venues to have shows that are accessible to people that aren't restrictive by age or cost.

Todd advances Yam's thoughts when he discusses the importance of actually living punk ideals, rather than just pontificating on them. Over the years at *Razorcake*, Todd had seen many business relationships falter because values did not align. He believed it took real deliberate attention to make sure that typical business practices never compromised punk ideology:

> It's bothersome that some of the most well-known people in DIY punk rock business are, oftentimes, can either walk away from it or that they are not providing a workable model for other people. I mean I understand it's hard to adapt person to person or place to place, there is always different variables, but being able to share those really good skillsets, I think is very important. I do appreciate people who can articulate what a perfect world would be for DIY punk. I think there is a time and a place for that, but their business practices do not always match what they were writing or saying. Some people gave up huge parts of their "autonomy" to a distributor or to someone else that they have no control over. Someone that is part of a larger mechanism and their punk enterprise got compromised because of that.

Todd continues to discuss the importance of punk ideals in business, specifically referring to the format of *Razorcake* (no corporate or major record label advertisements) as well as the political leanings of the content:

> All the parts really count, where they say that the medium is the message. Like what is being made is as important as what is being said. The format of the

zine is so important to me—like how the entire 'zine is put together—and then making sure there is no major label advertising and stuff. Because no matter how eloquently you write about something or how great your picture is, if its right up against something that's pretty onerous, then I'd feel like I'd failed putting this all together. So, for example, I just don't like Kid Rock. I think Kid Rock doing the American National Guard ad against (holds up an open 'zine) something Sean wrote just seems disingenious to me.

In addition to political convictions, many of the participants identified personal convictions related to an authentic and deliberate life. Aaron identified the "smart" ideals within punk. Even when he didn't fully understand all of the references, he learned to link the concepts of "smart" with "cool," which in turn had an impact on the ways in which Aaron viewed learning and education:

> Punk was something that I thought was cool, but it was clever and smart at the same time, so therefore I equated those things. So this was the first time that I thought something was cool and it was smart. It made me think.

Being "smart" was something that was relatively new to Aaron as he considered his hometown of Crystal Rover to be "vapid," where there "was just nothing to anything or anyone":

> Just that blank life.... You know you hate pop music, you hate sports, and you hate your teachers, but it all sort of blended together to be the same shit that I hate now as a 37-year-old man: subservient mediocrity. You know, bad art, bad food, bad company, bad jokes, bad humor—like subpar America. Punk rock was the antithesis of that. It was anything but subpar.

Similar to Aaron, Sean detailed the ways in which the political and the personal merged in his understanding of himself as a learner and as someone fully engaged in his life:

> I think in contemporary society, we are being trained to be consumers.... Basically that is the core of punk rock, how do you break free from the corporate control? The DIY punk community is about creating your own culture, don't consume someone else's culture, don't just take the shit that is sold to you or just dropped in your lap, make it organically and meaningful for you. This is your life, live in a full way. I think that matches what I learned in education and what I sought out in education, which is this is your life, this is your search for meaning, this is your search for enrichment, living an enriched life. Take an initiative in it, and I don't mean to take control, because it is well out of my control. But the things that are in my control, try to steer them in directions that are meaningful to me. The things that I can investigate, make them interesting to me; the things I can learn, make them enriching for me. Like, spiritually, intellectually enriching. I learned, if you

are really gonna understand literature, if you're really gonna understand writing, if you're really gonna understand fiction, go and engage with it. I think that's a combination of punk rock and my learning.

Aaron continues to reflect on the ways in which punk ideals and convictions pushed against what he experienced as a youth growing up in small-town Florida, yet he also acknowledges the pieces that fit well with who he was as a southerner:

> I would have to say, the way I was raised generally fits right alongside the core tenets of punk ethos: autonomy; respect for yourself and everyone else, as long as they deserve your respect; growth, celebrating personal growth and being a good person, a good human being and allowing those around you to be human beings. The things that my dad imparted to me as far as, "Hey, share what you got, keep what you need, help people out. Learn, don't stop learning—you see your brother fall, pick them up, help people out." It is not just art, it's political inclinations, it's moral inclinations, it's not just that we are into similar music, but we are of the same ilk. We want to believe that human beings should be able to be human beings no matter the color of their skin or gender of the person they love, that sort of shit; we are goddamn humanists.

Community

> *I much more prefer the idea of living in a community I helped to shape and foster, to living in a world where I do what people expect and end up feeling so isolated that I'm just wasting away. I learn so much more from this life than I was ever able to learn in a classroom, perhaps because I never quite felt myself or felt safe there, either. I need a good punk or DIY scene around me to live the life I want to live.*
>
> —Erin

> *I had hated my life in Crystal River up to that point. I still hated it. But now I felt like I wasn't alone.*
>
> —Aaron

The use of the word community was prevalent in most of the interview narratives. Although each punk learner detailed the ways in which community was defined, or was impactful for him or her, the consistency of the descriptor indicated the concept as a defining feature of the educative healing experience. In fact, for many punk learners, the feelings they experienced as a result of their engagement with their community was at the heart of their educative healing.

For a few of the punk learners, the community that was of importance to them was created through the experience of going on tour with their punk band. Yam describes his community as the

> people that we've known for years through playing with bands and setting up shows with them So everyone I hit up to help me, I've set a show up for or reviewed a record or helped them out with distribution. Or just been supportive in one way or another. So it's just like this reciprocation of favors. An endless game of favors; that's punk rock I guess.

Todd remarks on the very deliberate way he has structured *Razorcake* to be fully operated by volunteers from the Los Angeles community:

> We know what our limitations are. I mean Razorcake is not open to the public, but we are open to anybody that we can see eye to eye with and shows an interest in what we are doing. We have an open door. For example, we have a friend, Sam, who runs a record company; he is also a recording engineer who is gonna come and help us make our podcasts better. So having people help us and being able to replicate what they have told us is something I think we are really good at. It is so I can replicate what someone else has taught me and I can teach other people. We are kind of structured that way.

Aaron, who was also in a band that called Gainesville its home, addressed the construction and building of community through touring as evidenced by those he met and took care of him:

> I mean there are assholes everywhere, but being a young guy and going on tour and being cared for by complete strangers just because you have this mutual interest in punk rock—"Here eat my food, sleep in my house, shower in my shower, and listen to my records, and borrow my books." It's a special thing. I look around the room, and I'm like, "I remember being on tour with that guy!" and "I remember being in Portland, Oregon, and staying up all night in Las Cruces, New Mexico!" We are passing babies around and it is fucking beautiful. I feel so lucky to have that—that's worth something. We all met because we were into punk rock and now we have this community because of this thing before, but it still exists. Punk is something specific and always celebrated unity and community, in one way or another.

Like Aaron, Dave's engagement with Gainesville punk started at an early age; he articulated the shift away from the transient nature of the college town to one where a thriving community created a supportive infrastructure for punks:

> The Gainesville curse was that when your band would record, it would break up because someone was about to move away. There was such a short timeframe for people, but the people that were a few years older than me started

lingering around—started investing by buying homes or buying businesses—so that what they were doing could continue. I had no grand plans, but I liked it when I saw people doing that. The university brings a lot of new excited freshness to town and it snowballed; everyone adds to it and there aren't that many people who are taking away from it. So me and all the other like-minded people who enjoy music and are nice to people did the work to build an infrastructure.

Todd echoes the importance of contributing to the creation of a punk infrastructure in Los Angeles:

We donate 'zines to places that we would actually go to, not because we think it is strategically good to be there. So if it's a record store that we really like, bookstores that like us or we like them, I'm happy to do it. And its not so we can hopefully hook someone into buying more Razorcake, it's that we hope they can find something useful in that, hopefully they find something that resonates.

For three punk learners, their punk community engagement was a highly emotionally charged enterprise. Sean, an accomplished scholar and author, remarks on his loyalty to his punk community through his writing and teaching:

I publish all the time. My fifth book, which is my third novel, came out last June. I published a bunch of short stories recently in a university lit journal. I do all that publishing, but the most honest thing I write is my column for Razorcake, because it's for a community that I'm attached to deeply on an emotional level. The irony of anarchy and punk rock is that you want to support the individual, but to support the individual you have to support the community... you have to understand how communal the individual is. And you have to be communal, but it's individually empowering, and that gets at the root of DIY punk.

Aaron, in addition to being connected to a community while touring, also remarks about the ways he has become emotionally connected with those in his punk community and the solidarity that exists as a result. For Aaron, who described himself as an "outsider" during his life in school, he certainly found belonging in his punk community:

I mean everybody loves music. People that aren't into punk have a relationship with their music. Even older classic rock guys, I mean, their favorite band is The Who, I mean, I guarantee they've never had a beer with Pete Townsend. With punk, I've crossed paths with people I shouldn't have known, and crossed paths with bands that I shouldn't have known because it really is a community—it's a smaller community of people. That's one of the things punk affords its fans. I feel waves of pride and elation—ecstasy to a certain extent, a catharsis—especially when you are watching your friends, your buddies, your brothers make this beautiful noise, make this ruckus that is so much their own thing and it moves you. That's so fucking cool. I love being impressed and moved by my friends' art: that's punk.

For Erin, the community that punk offered her was a haven, a place she would retreat to during times of confusion and anger, a community where she could heal from her miseducative experiences:

It seems I often escaped from school or family problems into my punk artist life, but that is the life that feeds me and protects me. Through this large and thriving family and friend community, I have found both creative and utilitarian work that helps me pay for what I need to keep making art. My community shows me new music and art to keep me striving. It literally feeds us all through gardens and farms planted around town, and it gives us a safety network for when the world outside of the one, which we've built, weighs on us. Gainesville really was so punk—it was kind of wild—but even when it was wild, it was a community that took care of each other. Everybody really seemed like they loved each other and understood each other. Everybody looked like the island of misfit toys: we were all broke, we all had to work a ton to do anything. But when you were at a show together, everyone was doing the same thing: really excited and in a good mood. We were wild, but I found people that would care about me. So I threw myself into living with that group of people and this life.

Conclusion

In the preceding chapter, one possible set of phenomenological horizons was presented as grouped interpretations of the narrative data received through the in-depth interviews with six punk learners. Language to help frame these horizons was borrowed from John Dewey (1938/1997) and Kirsten Olson (2009), while the horizon descriptors were created after close readings of each set of interview transcripts. In the next chapter, Chapter 5, a discussion surrounding the transferability and relevance of these horizons using both Dewey and Olson, as well as the theoretical frameworks identified in Chapter 2, will be presented.

5

Discussion and Conclusion

> *We are always becoming ourselves and the self is not a preexisting unity to be discovered, but rather an ongoing project to be unfurled.*
> —Smith, Flowers, and Larkin, 2012, p. 389

In the preceding chapter, three phenomenological horizons were detailed using subthemes and were then contextualized further by referencing the work of Dewey (1938/1997) and Olson (2009), with the aim of explicating the main research question: What is the experience of adults who conceptualize their engagement with punk as educative? (as well as the subquestions) What role does punk play in learner self-confidence? What might punk engagement teach educators about perceptions of educative experiences?

As mentioned in Chapter 2, the theoretical framework that was intended to guide the data interpretation was three fold: public pedagogy (Giroux 2004, 2006, 2008; Sandlin, Schultz, & Burdik, 2010), social learning theory (Vygotsky, 1978), and self-directed learning (Grow, 1991). It is important to mention that these frameworks were originally chosen with a spectrum of data interpretation in mind, the interview protocol was developed with the aim to explore the experience of those who describe their engagement with punk as educative, and the framework set was to be used to analyze the ways in which the punk learners perceived these educative experiences.

While much of what the punk learners shared fell into a predicted spectrum surrounding their educative punk engagement, (i.e., inspirational lyrics, DIY ethos), what was unexpected were the ways in which the participants perceived what was in fact educative. After the interview transcriptions were closely read and coded using interpretive phenomenological analysis (IPA), the data revealed that punk learners interpreted their educative experience as less about content that was "learned" and more about who they were as learners while they were learning.

With this new path to consider, it was important to represent the punk learners' narratives well, which would require an additional framework-set that privileged their perceived learner self-concept, as well as the ways in which the punk learners' interpreted their educative engagement with punk as a form of educative healing. In this chapter, the horizons will be further discussed referencing the implications for education based on an analysis of these original theoretical constructs, but will also be extended through additional discussion using Dewey's work on miseducation and educative healing scholarship (Harrison, 2002; Holt, 2004; Noddings, 2003; Olson, 2009).

As Pinar articulates, curriculum can best be described as a "complicated conversation" whose educational point is "understanding the relations among academic knowledge, the state of society, the process of self-formation, and the character of the historical moment in which we live, in which others have lived, and in which our descendants will someday live" (Pinar, 2012, p. 187). Although the research analytic frameworks are not exclusively curricular based, I find it appropriate to pull from Pinar's since I am not sure there is a better use for education research than for the betterment of the ways in which learners experience curriculum in the most broad sense. What follows are scaffolded segments, where each analysis frame will engage in a "complicated conversation" with the data. This chapter will culminate in a summary with recommendations for further research.

Punk As: Public Pedagogy

Public pedagogy scholarship assists us in locating and seeing with new eyes the sites of learning that may significantly mark our learner-selves (Sandlin & Milam, 2008; Sandlin, Schultz, & Burdik, 2010), but are largely outside what is seen as the formal schooling structures. However, as Giroux, who is considered to be the originator of the term, articulates, the work of public pedagogy "invalidate the importance of schooling, it extends the sites of pedagogy" (Giroux, 2004, p. 498).

Public pedagogy is a fitting framework to analyze the narrative data present in my research as it brings to light spheres that foster educative or miseducative experiences equal to that of compulsory schooling. Giroux describes the notion that education and formal schooling have become synonymous in the public mind, yet in order for our goal of democracy to be reached, we have to broaden our understanding and definition of educative. This work to challenge the default connection between school and education,

> does not invalidate the importance of formal education to democracy, but it does require a critical understanding of how the work of education takes place in such institutions as well as in a range of other spheres such as advertising, television, film, the Internet, video game culture, and the popular press. (Giroux, 2004, p. 498)

Giroux does not mention punk culture specifically, but I would gather that the ideals and values of the punk DIY ethos, as defined by the research participants as well as punk scholarship, would fit nicely into the articulated vision of democracy that Giroux (2006) describes:

> Democracy cannot work if citizens are not autonomous, self-judging, and independent—qualities that are indispensable for students if they are going to make vital judgments and choices about participating in and shaping decisions that affect everyday life, institutional reform, and governmental policy. Pedagogy, in this instance, is put in the service of providing the conditions for students to invest in a robust and critical form of agency, one that takes seriously their responsibility to others, public life, and global democracy. Hence, pedagogy becomes the cornerstone of democracy in that it provides the very foundation for students to learn not merely how to be governed but also how to be capable of governing. (Giroux, 2006, p. 73)

With this in mind, it would be fitting for educators to explore, grapple with, and seek understanding of sites of learning that privilege and create the learning environments that nurture "critical forms of agency," as well as other indicators of democratic public pedagogy. Given the data collected, I would argue that engagement in punk, as perceived by participants, is one of these sites of learning. Table 5.1 outlines a few of the more poignant connections.

As stated by Sandlin, Schultz, and Burdik (2010), in their work on advancing public pedagogy scholarship, "We are constantly being taught, constantly learn, and constantly unlearn" (p. 1). If, as educators, we are to meet

TABLE 5.1 Public Pedagogy Evidence

Public Pedagogy	Transcripted Evidence
Critical Forms of Agency	"I'm not going to give in..." —Yam "Punk was about getting out there and being involved, doing something." —Sean "Punk Rock began to shatter the veil that was cast on me as a child." —Dave "Riot Grrl was hugely important to me because it embodied music, performance, art, zines, and activism—it shaped a lot of my early punk values." —Erin "That was the first time where I thought in other ways." —Todd "I started being very interested in punk Rock and literature—both things worked in tandem and made me think, 'School is bullshit, but that doesn't mean I have to give up.'" —Aaron
Responsibility to Others	"Me and all the other like-minded people who enjoy music and are nice to people did the work to build an infrastructure." —Dave "While I'm doing for someone else, there are people doing things for me that will make my life better." —Erin "It's something specific and always celebrated unity and community—in one way or another." —Aaron
Democratic Ideals	"I really came to understand that the essence of punk is equality." —Yam "DIY punk community is about creating your own culture." —Sean "Our community provides us with new music and art—it literally feeds us all through gardens and farms planted around town." —Erin "On the other side of that is that we do our part—hopefully suggesting to other people for them to do their part." —Todd

Public Pedagogy (in the Service of Democratic Agency) As Manifested in Punk Engagement

our obligation in providing educative experiences for learners, we must immerse ourselves in how learners experience "being taught," learning, and "unlearning." By using public pedagogy as a frame to ask learners to become experts on their own learning selves, we can become honest and open facilitators of the educative experience.

Punk As Social Learning Theory

As discussed in Chapter 2, social learning theory assumes that learners learn assisted through social interaction and experience. The social in social learning theory can be a flexible term, referring to a number of different sociological or interpersonal constructs. However, Lev Vygotsky, the Russian theorist who was responsible for the early writings on the subject, was largely concerned with the ways in which the learner developed as a result of the social experience. Vygotsky (1978) believed that learners existed within a zone of learning (otherwise knows as the zone of proximal development [ZPD], as detailed in Chapter 1), with an emphasis on the progression or development of understanding. According to Vygotsky, learning was not a static plateau that was reached with a demonstration of success, rather it was an ever-continuing cycle of mastery and interest that resulted in the steadily increasing of development. Much like a visual of an endless spiral staircase, each step of learning has it's own cyclical process; Vygotsky believed pace and the process of advancement were important aspects of the learning process.

Additionally important to this discussion, Vygotsky referenced the more knowledgeable other (MKO) as guiding the learning cycle to assist the learner's transition from interest to mastery to interest (with the cycle repeating). In terms of the narratives, evidence of social learning theory was present during the punk learners' initial interest in punk, as well in the stages of increased engagement (see Table 5.2).

Engagement in punk was purely voluntary for the punk learners, and their access occurred at various points in their lives and within the punk community (i.e., music on the radio, friends, neighbors, shows). Interestingly, at each point in which social learning theory could be traced to a transcripted perception of an experience, there appeared to be an advent of increased engagement in punk. In other words, when a punk learner could articulate their experience using language that could be ascribed to social learning theory, his/her participation in punk increased, as well as his/her understanding of an empowered and independent learner self-concept. As a visual, one way these movements could be further explored is to locate them within Grow's (1991) self-directed learning rubric.

Punk As: Self-Directed Learning

Grow (1991) discussed the importance of being able to assess where a learner was on the spectrum of self-directedness, so that the teaching environment would not only match that of the learner, but also nurture a development toward a more advanced place along the spectrum. In some ways, Grow's model for ideal education is aligned with Vygotsky's ZPD model. For Grow, when learners are advancing through the self-directed learning rubric, ideally it is because the learning environment and the teacher are well matched for the learner's development pace. Although the punk learner narratives correlate with all four stages of Grow's self-directed learning

TABLE 5.2 Social Learning Theory Evidence

Social Learning Theory Represented in Educative Punk Engagement	
Learners are prone to learn through the imitation of models and examples of activism and behavior they see in social scenarios.	"As weird as everybody looked to me, it felt fucking awesome. I mean everything I can think to say sounds cliché, but I knew I wanted to be a part of it for sure—for the first time, it felt totally affirming." —Aaron "So after Minor Threat—Ian MacKeye started Fugazi—everything was deliberate, all shows were 5 dollars, every record was on Dischord records. To me, that's very deliberate—I have a vision for the world, I'm gonna live my life according to this vision." —Sean
Learners can quickly decode the behavior/consequence relationship for learner behavior, belief, and actions.	"I try to work on things, instead of being negative about things—like fuck school, fuck my professor, because when those people are gone and you are out of those situations, its up to you to make best thing you possibly can." —Todd "Being near Gainesville, you see it kind of perfectly with Var at No Idea—No Idea has always been intentional about everything they do and they have been very successful about that—and Var has created an incredible scene in Gainesville." —Sean "And you cant be a jerk If you are not a jerk, you can do anything in the DIY world." —Dave
Learning happens before and after physical/intellectual development, they are interconnected at all levels	"I remember writing down words and thinking, 'I guess I'm spelling it right' and I'd look up words I didn't know. Pixies are the first band that came to mind—I remember listening to the Pixies and looking up unfamiliar vocabulary." —Aaron "Finding punk Rock was like fun detective work." —Todd "If you are really gonna understand literature, if your really gonna understand writing, if your really gonna understand fiction—go and engage with it." —Sean "7 Seconds took that exact same thought pattern and feeling and logic and anger and turned it positive to building instead destroying. Or destroying in order to build." —Dave
References to a More Knowledgeable Other (MKO)	"Literature and punk were parts of the same thing for me—it was the outside world for me. It was the bigger, better outside of my own Crystal River existence." —Aaron "Picking up fanzines when I could, trying to be as informed as possible, like picking up used cassettes." —Todd "The head of the college radio station lived next door to me and so we shared a porch and so and she'd always be telling me about new bands and turning me on to new stuff and so basically the house where I lived was the campus radio station house." —Sean

spectrum, their engagement with punk was most aligned with the last three levels: interested, involved, and self-directed.

Grow describes the Level 2 Interested (see Table 5.3) as being best served with a motivating guide as the teacher. In the case of each participant, the very first engagement with punk rock largely came in the form of music lyrics that sparked interest, intrigue, and curiosity.

As the punk learners further developed their engagement within punk, they became involved, where the learning environment and the "teacher," which could have taken on a number of forms, acted more as equals. The concept of learning from peers was consistently discussed in each narrative

TABLE 5.3 Self-Directed Learning Development Level Two Evidence

Punk Learner	Transcript	Notes
	Level Two: Interested	
Aaron	"It was 6th grade when I first discovered punk Rock. I met this kid who gave a dubbed copy of the Dead Milkmen's first record Big Lizard in My Backyard."	Friend as MKO
Dave	"I first heard punk Rock in my dad's machine shop. That got me started on my quest for all things kick-ass, this was around the same time I had the feeling of wanting to express my own independence."	Co-worker as MKO
Erin	"My skipping school had me hanging out at the record store and stuff so that's how I got into knowing punk kids. The music was hugely important to my artistic process."	
Sean	"I started listening to punk Rock music when I was 15 or 16. Would go over to my friends and we would always tape 120 Minutes on MTV—that's where we'd learn about punk bands."	Television as MKO
Todd	"So I started writing and I listened to more punk Rock—something that angry was awesome to me because my head was so out of whack. That radio station, KUNV, was hugely influential. It was literally like when I went to sleep I would just hit record and I would listen to those tapes with the PSAs and all."	College Radio Station as MKO
Yam	"The first time I listened to punk Rock was in 4th grade. I think I did the Columbia House 16 CDs for a penny—I did that 3 times."	Yam later identified that his interest increased dramatically in 9th grade when he understood the political ideology within underground punk.

and detailed in the horizons affirmation and community; the involved level of self-directed learning (see Table 5.4) could clearly be seen in the ways the punk learners described the transition from listening to punk music on the radio or on found mix-tapes to attending punk shows and befriending those in punk bands.

Level 4: Self-Directed is described by Grow as "engaged work with individual projects" (p. 129). Each punk learner interviewed discussed their level of engagement at this Level 4 through their do-it-yourself (DIY) creation. This self-directed creation manifested externally through Yam and

TABLE 5.4 Self-Directed Learning Development Level Three Evidence

	Level Three: Involved	
Punk Learner	Transcript	Notes
Aaron	"The first time I went to Gainesville, I think I was 14—that was when I really caught the punk Rock bug. I went to that first Radon show at the Hardback with my buddy that had a learner's permit."	Aaron later discusses the impact that Radon had on his life as he became friends with the band members.
Dave	"Any time I would encounter something in literature or music that was destroying the bullshit fabric in a different way—I would gravitate towards it—relentlessly. After that, I couldn't get music fast enough. When I like something, I want to know everything about it, everything associated with it. I would read the liner notes of the CDs and go find everything that was mentioned."	For Dave, involvement was connected to a political ideology
Erin	"In Gainesville, there were three places where I would see the punk shows that really shaped me: Common Grounds, Wayward Council and the Ark."	
Sean	"I tried a couple of times to set up a reading series in Tallahassee. I would try to write about the punk shows that I would go to. A friend of mine worked at Kinko's and we made little 'zines that we passed out."	
Todd	"When I was living and going to school in Arizona, I'd go to a fair amount of punk Rock shows, but Flagstaff, you know, there wasn't a lot going on. So during college, we would go down to Phoenix to go see shows."	
Yam	"It was around this time that I found the band, Dillinger Four – their lyrics broke walls down for me. I knew punk was political, but now I knew it wasn't only raising your fist and waving a flag, but it was also thinking, 'I'm not going to give in…'" and having strong personal and political convictions."	For Yam, the advanced involvement was markedly internal

Dave's music, Erin's artwork, and Sean and Todd's punk 'zine. Aaron, Yam, and Erin also noted internal manifestations through a creation of a more confident self; in other words, punk engagement increased the belief in themselves that they could create. Grow also indicates that learners who have reached the highest level of self-direction are aware of their learning style and abilities, and can gauge when and how they will learn best. Many punk learners discussed this learner self-concept awareness early on as a young learner, yet it was also clearly advanced through their engagement with punk (see Table 5.5).

Self-directed learning, as evidenced by traits such as competent, productive, and independent is a clearly articulated goal in many facets of the United States educational system. Academic think tanks report on self-directed learning, school district mottos aim for it, teacher lesson plans require evidence of it. Demonstrations of self-directed learning are woven into both the rhetoric and pragmatic structures of schooling. With this said, there is no shortage of academic scholars that criticize these same schooling structures, accusing the systems of schooling, at all levels, to be built on tenets of obedience, compliance, and conformity (see Darder, Baltodano & Torres, 2008; McLaren & Kincheloe, 2007), which are the antithesis of the culture of self-direction.

These accusations leave educators with the task of considering this question: What is the environment or culture that nurtures and perpetuates self-directed learning, if not for the current system of compulsory schooling? Even at its best and most liberal, compulsory schools are still accused of limiting the scope of what and how students are able to learn. If self-directed learning is a critical component of schooling despite the curriculum or format, then how might learners become more self-directed in other capacities of their lives?

The narratives of the punk learners within my research did not concretely discern a linear path; this showcased their process of becoming a self-directed learner. Rather, it is my interpretation that each participant had a spectrum of self-direction already oriented within them before they were miseducated. In accordance to how Grow describes his rubric, learners may progress to become more self-directed, once the environment and teacher is specifically fitting for their individual path; this was evidenced by each participant as they grew from first being interested in punk, to being involved through a variety of ways based on their interests and skill-set, to finally achieving self-direction in their pursuits and creation. This final level not only exists to keep the learner sustained and with a sense of accomplishment, but also, for each participant, serves as a way to contribute

TABLE 5.5 Self-Directed Learning Development Level Four Evidence

Level Four: Self-Directed

Punk Learner	Transcript	Notes
Aaron	"So I started taking charge of my own learning. I started being very interested in punk Rock and literature. I thought, 'Hey, you are getting shafted here, you need to pay attention to the world, and you need to try to learn.'"	DIY Creation = learner Self-Concept
Dave	"Since I was 16, so in 20 years, there have only been a few months when I wasn't in an active band. The most notable band I have been is Grabass Charlestons—who are now The Careeners. The most recent time I performed was two days ago."	DIY Creation = Band Participation
Erin	"One of the most defining moments for me was when my friends in FIYA asked me to create the artwork for a band shirt. It was important for me to create for them; it was the first work I did for a band that I thought was legitimate—it made me feel legitimate."	DIY Creation = Artwork
Sean	"I started a publishing company as a construction worker—that's about as DIY as it gets. I didn't know anything about publishing, but I figured, 'Fuck, do it yourself! You want to know how to publish? Go to the library and get a book and learn how to publish.'"	DIY Creation = Publishing
Todd	"When I was working at Flipside, I wanted to really throw myself into punk. Not only going to shows, but writing live reviews of those shows. Not only listening to some music, but hundreds and hundreds of records. I wanted to immerse myself, and educate myself, so I was intentionally trying to take in as much as possible. It was my self-education."	DIY Creation = Publishing
Yam	"Punk helped me understand that it was okay to be yourself—to understand that we are all doing what we can and we all have to get by somehow. It was at the same time that I started to create...because all of a sudden I felt that I could create. punk told me that even though I wasn't in this flashy band and I wasn't this high profile person, I could still set up shows, create 'zines..."	DIY Creation = Zines, setting up shows

to their chosen community, as a way to aid in its survival so it can meet the needs of others.

Herein lies an important question: If self-direction is the ultimate goal of educators and will also result in a gratifying sense of empowerment for the learner, then in what ways can we, as professional educators, contribute

TABLE 5.6 Self-Directed Learning Commonalities Within Punk Engagement

Commonalities of the Path Toward a Self-Directed Learner Self-Concept via Punk Engagement	
Opportunities to identify, explore, understand, and honor a learner self-concept	Perceived opportunities for creative self-expression that derive from individual interests
Events which affirm lived experience, learner self-concept, or other identity	Engagement in a community which fosters solidarity, acceptance and comradery
Engagement in a learning space that is perceived as safe from judgment or callousness.	Freedom to imagine or determine physical, intellectual or emotional pursuits

to a society where learners have access to the environment and teacher (in whatever form they may present as) required for their particular process? Of course, there are many assumptions regarding the aims of education made prior to the creation of this question; yet, if we can agree to the previous terms, then I would argue that each participant's path to create or reclaim an empowered self-directed learner self-concept had commonalities (Table 5.6) that may be of use as educators attempt to answer the aforementioned question.

In addition to the these commonalities, I found that the punk learner narratives also indicated that the self-directed learner self-concept was enhanced when there were no miseducative experiences to navigate simultaneously. For instance, Yam, Aaron, and Erin's progression toward self-direction were substantially increased once their formal compulsory schooling was complete. Additionally, Dave, Todd, and Sean found that their self-directed learner self-concept could be based on their own interests, rather than being confined or limited to surviving or navigating their miseducative experiences. This is not to say that miseducative experiences do not present themselves often throughout a lifetime, yet I would imagine there to be a balance that still affords a learner the time and energy to nurture an empowered and confident learner self-concept. In other words, these commonalities are not the whole of the path to self-direction, but rather are a piece of the process, which will include several variables.

If I was asked to offer anything to Grow's self-directed rubric, it would be to add a fifth level: contribution. If there is much to be learned or applied from this analysis, it is that self-directed learning, or DIY ethos as it was often referred to in the interview transcripts, is best understood in a social arena that is reciprocal. When reviewing the data (Table 5.7), it appeared that the internal motivation that inspired self-directed learning was

TABLE 5.7 Self-Directed Learning Development Proposed Level Five Evidence

	Proposed Level Five: Contribution	
Punk Learner	Transcript	Notes
Aaron	"I love my friends, I am so proud of my friends—the circle that I have. It is because of punk because when I met all these folks, that was the tie that bound us all together. Everything is shared, advice is shared, babysitting is shared, resources are shared."	Community Contribution
Dave	"I started working at No Idea Records in 1996—just helping them assemble 'zine and CD packages. Gainesville is a special place. Now, there are a plethora of places that take good care of touring bands and plenty of places for bands to practice where the cops won't shut them down. We have built all of that over the last 20 years."	punk Infrastructure Contribution
Erin	"I get to be part of this community where I can be an artist. I can be involved in community things. I want to be involved. My friends are all doing things that I am excited about and I get to be a part of that."	Community Contribution
Sean	"Now I can take some of these ideas from punk Rock and bring them into my classes. I didn't want them to be too dogmatic—I didn't want them to be intrusive—but rather, I wanted them to help empower kids. I think that punk values are good values for kids."	Ideologic Contribution
Todd	"I kind of liken it to the idea that Razorcake is a bunch of bricks—and the bricks represent our DIY punk community of people's work with us, but those bricks need to be formed into a bridge—we form that structure. Missing any of those people's hard work, we would be incomplete."	Publishing Contribution
Yam	"Punk is productivity and doing things that require as little environmental energy and resources as possible. It also should be accessible and affordable—which is another form of access. In my life now, I try to never leave that train of thought. I'm always in a band, always working on a zine—I struggle to set up shows any way I can."	Infrastructure Contribution

described as the result of an interplay between participant and the learning environment, as well as a teacher. These social exchanges continue to exist despite the achievement of a self-directed level; therefore, for these apt environments and teachers to continue to exist for additional learners, then a contribution from the self-directed learner would be a way for their "projects and engaged work" to directly assist in the maintenance of a thriving site of learning. Specifically for those in the punk community, it is not enough to be merely self-directed; for each of the participants, it was even more important to give back to that community and make sure it is sustained.

Role of Miseducation

> *What avail is it to win prescribed amounts of information about geography and history, to win ability to read and write, if in the process the individual loses his own soul?*
> —Dewey, 1938/1997, p. 26

Much has been written about the educational experience, specifically schooling experience, which has been thought to be harmful for the learner. Whether it is racist school structures (see Hyland, 2005; Kailin, 1994; Lewis, 2001; Seidl, 2007; Spring, 2012; Valenzuela, 1999), oppressive and insensitive curriculum (see Au, 2014; Gay, 2000; Knauss, 2009; Sleeter, 2000), inadequate facilities (see Schneider, 2002; Uline & Tschannen-Moran, 2008); or teacher retention (see Cowen & Winters, 2013; Ronfeldt, Loeb, & Wyckoff, 2012), the desire to analyze and isolate that which troubles the formal schooling system in the United States has long been fervent. Additionally, there is scholarship exploring what may be harmful to learners, but falls outside of the realm of the school building (see Jackson, Vann, Kotch, Pahel, & Lee, 2011; McWhirter, Ramos, & Medina, 2013; Milner, 2013).

In terms of locating the responsible structures for learner stagnation, struggle, or apathy, the question of the best ways to engage a learner have been the subject of education theoretical dialogue for centuries. What exactly fosters learning? How do we know when something has been learned? How might we respond to a learner who appears disengaged or disinterested? What is the role of the learner and the teacher? Educators and scholars have had varied answers over several generations, and yet we continue to ask these same questions.

Of what does Dewey's construct of miseducation assist in answering these questions? Dewey, in *Experience and Education*, claims that all education is experiential, but not all experience is educational. In fact, there are many experiences that are miseducative and they deter or stunt further learning. Dewey views experience and education as being constructed by interaction and continuity. "The two principles of continuity and interaction are not separate from each other. They intercept and unite. They are, so to speak, the longitudinal and lateral aspects of experience" (p. 44). Interaction is the experience, the interplay between the learner and his environmental ecology. Continuity is how this interaction contributes to the expansion of the learner's willingness to engage in future learning opportunities:

> As an individual passes from one situation to another, his world, his environment, expands and contracts... what he has learned in the way of knowledge and skill in one situation becomes an instrument of understanding and dealing effectively with the situations that follow. This process goes on as long as life and learning continue. (Dewey, 1938/1997, p. 44)

Miseducative experience is sourced from damaging interactions that disrupt the continuity of learning. Dewey primarily focused on the miseducative within the formal traditional schooling mentality that he was concerned with during the early 20th century; however, his discussion on miseducation, I believe, can be applied to educative experiences that fall outside of the school as well. Dewey perceived learning as the "formation of enduring attitudes," which were more important than the actual content to be learned, because "the most important attitude that can be formed is that of the desire to go on learning" (Dewey, 1938/1997, p. 48). It is this attitude that is crushed during repeated miseducative experiences.

As detailed in Chapter 3, each participant recalled experiences that would be defined by Dewey as miseducative, many were located within schooling structures, but others were not. The interaction of the miseducative experience was with a system of trust, but not always a school. No matter where it occurred, the miseducative experience (Table 5.8) disrupted the continuity of learning through impacting the learners' attitude of themselves as learners or tainting the learning material or matter in such a way that it was felt as defeating to the learner.

The traumatic consequences of miseducative experiences for the punk learners are not unlike the students who have been and remain the concern of educators, who continue to seek answers to the questions surrounding the nature of learning. Nearly every education researcher and scholar has articulated the ways in which students suffer under one schooling shortcoming or another. Yet few scholars intimately address what remedies the students have as resources (outside of schooling) to address their miseducation; oftentimes it is suggested that a different form of schooling/school (i.e., alternative schooling, charter schools, college prep, international baccalaureate, gifted and talented programs) is the answer to all the ills students' bear.

I would not argue that a purely educative experience, as defined by Dewey, could not be a remedy for miseducation. But given the particular

TABLE 5.8 Prepunk Miseducative Experiences

Prepunk Miseducative Experiences

Punk Learner	Interaction	Continuity
Aaron	"I remember I had some horrible teachers. I had a math teacher, Ms. Brooks, in the 7th grade. She knew that I didn't know the answer and I couldn't do the work. She didn't like me."	"It made me feel like, 'Fuck this, fuck these teachers, I don't need this anyway.' It definitely made me start to resent education and think negatively."
Dave	"He (Geraldo) had this line about human sacrifice and blood drinking, and my brain says, 'Huh, that sounds exactly like a catholic mass, why is one thing okay, and one thing horrible.' My brain started seeing the social view of things that I saw as hypocritical.	"I was angry, frustrated. I wanted to smash the state and tell the Vatican to piss off. I became anti-establishment."
Erin	"I had a really strict chemistry teacher—I had messed up some homework and I was trying to talk to her about it, and she was like 'I know you are just a liar'—she had heard from my 10th grade teachers about me—and she was like, 'I know that you are bad.'"	"It just made me want to stop going. I was just like, 'Well, fuck it—I don't want to go to school anymore.' Looking back, it seems like a natural progression of just giving up."
Sean	"I had this one teacher she was this fire and brimstone evangelical and she was convinced that half the kids in the class were satanic. She would say, 'I cant deal with you kids, I'm just gonna write the notes on the board and you guys can just copy them down.' We'd never talk about it, we'd never process it. We'd be tested on it later."	"So what made school suck for me? Everything that they are pushing toward now in education. I mean multiple-choice tests even for a 9 year old I think I could just see that was a waste of my time."
Todd	"I remember not being great at school. I know I was a slow learner at the beginning, I was a slow reader and then it really clicked like in 1st or 2nd grade."	"For some reason I just feel so distant. I am not good at this type of testing. Its very difficult for me, it makes me very anxious and I'm not good at it. I don't like thinking that way. I'm not naturally gifted at learning, I'm just not a talented guy that way."
Yam	"Year after year, I would get put in the dumb kid class. I felt like there was just so much busy work that was constantly being put upon you to complete and that there is just no reason to do it other than to keep you in the classroom."	"I always hated school and never really appreciated it or enjoyed it even My mentality was: I have to get done with school—my goal is to be done with school forever."

scope of my research, the narratives offered by the punk learners convey that they were attracted to particular kinds structures, and none of them were school-based. Rather, after the participants were influenced by miseducative experiences along a spectrum of trauma (some experiences appeared to be perceived as navigable, while others cut through their humanity and left a deep mark), it was the educative healing of punk engagement that was a salve. The educative healing experienced through the engagement with punk acted as a catalyst for the participant to restore, and in some instances create, what they interpreted as a stronger and empowered learner self-concept. In fact, it is this educative healing that I believe is the crux, or the phenomenological essence, of the educative experience of punk engagement.

Role of Educative Healing

> *It is the quality of our experiences, the satisfaction, excitement, or joy that we get or fail to get from them, that will determine how those experiences change us—in short, what we learn.*
> —Holt, 2004, p. 13

For Dewey, an experience is educational when it "arouses curiosity, strengthens initiative, and sets up desires and purposes that are sufficiently intense to carry a person over dead places in the future" (Dewey, 1938/1997, p. 38). For the punk learners, many of their prepunk educational experiences, if we are to commit Dewey's definition, consisted of out-of-school experiences. Both Aaron and Sean described their best learning to have come from their job sites—marina and construction, respectively. Erin's solitude and freedom to draw, and Dave's time with the Boy Scouts accounted for educative experiences that inspired their curiosity and increased their confidence. Based on their prepunk educative experiences, participants entered into their individual set of miseducative experiences with an emerging sense of a learner self-concept, yet for each participant, these miseducative experiences necessitated healing in order for their learner self-concept to advance through the levels of self-direction.

The concept of a healing process is prevalent in spiritual, physical, and mental health scholarship (see Deegan, 2002; Ventegodt, Andersen, & Merrick, 2003;); as well as organizational theory (Powley & Piderit, 2008). In terms of punk-based scholarship, Mageary's doctoral research on hardcore punk identity formation is of special interest to my research, as he locates what he describes as *"small t" therapy* within punk engagement:

"Small t" therapy is a self-constructed healing experience; a chance to acknowledge and confront old wounds and make progress on the path towards self actualization without necessarily entering into the mental health system or engaging in the medical models of treatment. In the context of hardcore punk, this is an embodied process in which movement (at shows) and participation (in the scene) are prioritized. (Mageary, 2001, p. 209)

For the interest of this education theory based research discussion, I pursued scholarship that put forth ideas that appear to advance the ways in which Dewey defined educative with an emotional focus on healing. I first went to Olson (2009), who is one of few education scholars who explicitly use the term healing, to review her work detailing the wounds schooling inflicts upon students and their families. Olson provides four stages of healing, Table 5.9 outlines the stages as well as connects them with participant data:

Much of Olson's work is oriented in proactive methods or preparation for the school that wounds. Olson has several recommendations for ways in which students have been able to heal themselves, as well as suggestions for how parents, teachers, and peers can aid in the healing process. For instance, Olson details "what elementary and middle school students need to survive school" (Olson, 2009, pp. 154–155), as well as "demystifying" the learner type of students so that they have a great sense of "learner self-knowledge" (p. 146) that will aid them in navigating school environments. Lastly, Olson discusses her own parenting as a form of preparation by assisting her children in adopting what she describes as "stances" (p. 150), where they can attempt to remain actualized and empowered individuals within oppressive school systems and beyond into their adult lives.

Olson's work can only provide analysis for a piece of the participants' educative engagement in punk; therefore, I also looked to John Holt, an education scholar best known for his advocacy of alternative education. Holt does not explicitly use the term healing in his work, yet he describes at length the ways in which people can find joy and purpose (a key Deweyan requirement for education) in their life pursuits, by destroying the "cover" of the schooling system, which tells society that its aim is to lift up students, all the while it is keeping them down (Holt, 2004, p. 8).

As part of his work, Holt starts with questioning the language that is used in the education field; he casts aside the term "learner," and instead favors "doer." He perceives the largest difference between the two is the most crucial element of the empowerment process: freedom of choice. According to Holt, it is as a doer that we may engage in "self-directed, purposeful, meaningful life and work," instead of what the term "education"

TABLE 5.9 Stages of Healing Evidence

Stages of Healing School Wounds (Olson, 2009)

Stage	Interpretation	Transcript Data
1. Self-blame and private shame	The emotional hardships of being wounded by schooling—associated with shame, embarrassment, guilt, dissonance, disappointment, and depression. The student blames themselves for their perceived failures and hides them.	"It made me feel ashamed to not do well." —Erin "I guess that was when I became a poor learner." —Dave "I was angry, I remembered being angry." —Aaron "I was just stuck in school. I was bored." —Sean "I am not good at that type of testing. I fail . . . " —Todd
2. Points of Light and Moments of Insight	The experiences that bring "unexpected success or validation." Seeing past the old labels and knowing that there is more to learning then the past wounds.	"It made me feel legitimate." —Erin "I thought, 'I need this—I am about this.' The imagery was exactly how I was feeling." —Dave "So I started taking charge of my own learning." —Aaron "To me, punk was about getting out there and being involved, doing something. Don't sit at home and complain. Don't get bored." —Sean "I wanted to immerse myself, and educate myself." —Todd
3. Grieving: Anger and Sadness	Coming to terms with the anger, sadness, rage, and frustration over the wounding. Resolving the blame associated with teachers or schools which have wounded.	"Looking back, I have often escaped from school or family problems into my punk artist life, but that is the life that feeds me and protects me." —Erin "I remember that I didn't feel as tragic about it anymore. I felt empowered." —Aaron "It also gave me confidence to do other things." —Todd
4. Reconciliation: Activism and Engagement in Change	"Committing to the reform of the institution of education at some level, either as teacher, administrator, political activist, or reformer" (111)	So after I received my PhD and when I got on the tenure track at Channel Island, I knew I could actually be deliberate about curriculum. Now I can take some of these ideas from punk Rock and bring them into my classes. – Sean

has become known to be: "learning cut off from active life and done under pressure of bribe or threat, greed and fear" (Holt, 2004, p. 3).

> Next to the right to life itself, the most fundamental of all human rights is the right to control our own minds and thoughts. That means, the right to decide for ourselves how we will explore the world around us, think about our own and other persons' experiences, and find and make the meaning of our own lives. Whoever takes that right away from us, as educators do, attacks the very center of our being and does us a most profound and lasting injury. He tells us, in effect, that we cannot be trusted even to think, that for all our lives, and that any meaning we may make for ourselves, out of our own experience, has no value. (Holt, 2004, p. 4)

Holt, like Dewey, understands that miseducation can be damaging to the learner psyche, creating dependence on an educational system that defines their value and measures their potential. According to Holt, whose "concern is not to improve education, but to do away with it" (Holt, 2004, p. 4), the best way for a person to be self-directed and assured in their actions was to forego the label learner, which has been co-opted by an "inhumane" schooling system and, instead become a doer:

> By "doing" I do not mean only things done with the body, the muscles, with hands and tools, rather than with the mind alone. I am not trying to separate or put in opposition what many call the "physical" or the "intellectual." Such distinctions are unreal and harmful. Only in words can the mind and body be separated. In reality they are one; they act together. So by "doing," I include such actions as talking, listening, writing, reading, thinking, even dreaming. (Holt, 2004, p. 5)

I found Holt's framework of the doer to be especially apt in the discussion surrounding punk engagement as educative healing. Holt describes doers as those who "are allowed, encouraged, and helped to work with and help each other, and to think, talk, write, and read about the things that most excite and interest them" in an effort to "direct and control their own lives' (Holt, 2004, p. 7). This doer self-concept can be seen in the description of the fourth level of self-direction (Grow, 1991) and the do-it-yourself (DIY) creation phenomenological horizon detailed in Chapter 3, where punk learners reveled in their independent spirit. Both Holt and Dewey asserted that it is through the empowered curiosity and creativity, as well as having the room to actualize these desires, that feeds the drive to continue learning as a lifelong learner. In other words, the more we as empowered people connect with the parts of our selves that do and create, the more we are in touch with our best learner self-concept.

When seen through Holt's frame, the educative engagement in punk would be one way for punk learners to be able to "nourish and encourage these [doer] qualities, so that even if they learn little or nothing in school, they can continue the learning they were doing so well before they went to school" (Holt, 2004, p. 8). As I interpret it, Holt believes that it is from the reconstructing of what it means to be a learner (to equate it with the empowered doer self-concept, rather than the system which miseducates) that will authentically nurture a self-directed person who can freely pursue their goals and contribute to a healthier society (Table 5.10). Although Holt is specifically referring to schooling systems as the main source of miseducative experiences, in my research, miseducation is presented in a number of ways and not just through schooling. Despite the location of the miseducative experience (which may or may not be important, this would have to be established through additional research), they still traumatize and stall an empowered, self-directed learner self-concept. If we are to believe that all experiences contribute to how we perceive ourselves, then we must be able to recognize the miseducation that is sourced outside of school as well.

As I continued to push out my understanding of the depths of educative healing scholarship, I was also drawn to the writings of Steven Harrison, consciousness scholar, whose work aligns with renowned education scholar Nel Noddings, in that they both write about the role of happiness in education. To expand on both of these scholars, it is important to note that they approach the ways in which happiness is an important part of education and crucial to the learning process a bit differently (Table 5.11). Noddings

TABLE 5.10 "Doer" As Healing Evidence

Evidence of "Doer" Learner Self-Concept as Healing

Punk Learner	Transcript
Aaron	"After I was deeply, deeply into punk Rock, I started taking charge of my own learning."
Dave	"I can see a way around anything. You just need to see it in a different capacity. If you have an idea of an end result, you can do it. So as long as you know the goal and visualize it—then you go do it."
Erin	"It was important for me to create. Music was hugely important to my artistic process—and the DIY values were always there."
Sean	"Get involved, do something. Don't sit at home and complain go out and create."
Todd	"I'd never done anything just to do it before. I'd always only done work if it was assigned to me. That was the first time where I thought in other ways. Creative writing and drawing were two big things that I lucidly remember starting to do."
Yam	"We release our own records—we don't really approach other record labels to release stuff for us, we feel more comfortable doing it ourselves."

(2003) primarily concerns her work with the ways in which schools can promote happiness as a central educational aim as preparation for both private/home life and democratic public life. Harrison (2002) is more concerned with the learner self-concept surrounding happiness as it is manifests as a form of democratic agency. Both scholars believe that schools are sources of miseducative experiences, that they nearly "kill curiosity and creativity" (Noddings, 2003, p. 31) and that the "institutionalized educational bureaucracy" is largely tasked with "coerced learning" rather than self-directed initiative (Harrison, 2002, p. 39).

Although, my research has less to do with potential ways to repair schooling, their scholarship is helpful in discussing educative punk engagement as healing, since they address emotional needs as a form of and a

TABLE 5.11 Happiness As Healing Evidence

	Evidence of Happiness in Learner Self-Concept as Healing
Productivity and Happiness	"Punk is productivity." —Yam
	"The whole idea was be active." —Sean
	"There was never anyone making me feel bad about myself." —Erin
	"I want to know everything about it, everything associated with it." —Dave
The Intentional Family	"I wanted to be on that team, I wanted to be on that side." —Aaron
	"This band that I respected so much were my friends and were accessible to me." —Erin
	"So me and all the other like-minded people who enjoy music and are nice to people did the work." —Dave
	"By then I'd been around punk for 10 years and I knew my tribe." —Sean
Living Community	"The bricks represent our DIY punk community of people's work." —Todd
	"I much prefer the idea of living in a community I helped shape and foster." —Erin
	"Gainesville is a special place." —Dave
	"I remember moving to Gainesville and realizing that I was surrounded by interesting and smart people." —Aaron
Learning Community	"I get to be part of this community where I can be an artist." —Erin
	"That was another way that I built relationships with punk organizers in their own towns." —Dave
	"We would set up readings there and get people to come out to readings and perform them." —Sean
	"We also educate." —Todd
	"It definitely made being smart cool. I could tell that knowledge was a good thing." —Aaron

144 ■ DIY Punk As Education

catalyst for education. Harrison believes that it is through educating the "whole" child that learning flourishes:

> This is precisely why the systems of education that we have are failing. They are systems based only on information and thinking conceptually about that information. Thinking is a useful tool, but it always breaks the whole into parts and can never entirely synthesize the parts into the essential whole. (Harrison, 2002, p. 45)

When we "become whole," we are healing the broken parts of ourselves. It is through a desire to be happy in an education structure, and also happy with ourselves as learners, that we seek to be engaged in sites of learning that authenticate our happiness (Table 5.11); we find healing in environments that tell us that we deserve to be happy, healed, whole learners:

> The best homes and schools are happy places. The adults in these happy places recognize that one aim of education is happiness. They also recognize that happiness is a mean and an end. Happy children, growing in their understanding of what happiness is, will seize their educational opportunities with delight, and they will contribute to the happiness of others. (Noddings, 2003, p. 261)

Harrison (2002) describes the happy child learner as one that is engaged in a site of learning that embodies the following constructs: productivity and happiness, intentional family, living community, and learning community.

Summary and Future Research

Education research is concerned with that which is the most human of our existence: How do we make meaning of the world around us? How do we construct thought? How do we learn? What is worth knowing? To what end is learning important? I interpret education and learning as a sacred act, one that is as mysterious as it is elusive. There is no way to come to just one complete understanding of the mind, and the ways in which we use it, to "become" or to "do." Our wonder into the nature of learning has been, and will continue to be, a driving force to understand others and ourselves.

For as long as we have had a formal system of education, we have been concerned with the good it can do for students, communities, and our society, but we have also been troubled by the costs. Clearly, practitioners and scholars have noted that students and communities have not always been treated well by schooling systems, specifically those whose experiences do not reflect the dominant hegemony (see Burkholder, 2011; Spring, 2012a,

2012b; Tyack, 1974), yet the public mind continues to believe that education is the "great equalizer" that Horace Mann once proclaimed it was.

Yet, it is a different Mann quote that guides my closing thoughts: "Education prevents both the revenge and the madness" (Mann, 1840/1989, p. 60). Mann believed that education brought enlightenment to the mind and body, that it produced the ability to reason and understand the world in such a way that people would not be held captive by the unknown. When we became educated, we could move beyond any obstacle; we knew that there was more to the world and society than our very immediate ecology, which may present as challenging. If we were educated, nothing was finite.

Like Mann, I imagine education to be a state of being, rather than a set of concrete facts to be memorized; the ability to critically think should be the ultimate goal of education. I appreciate that Harrison (2002) reminds us that thinking is not enough to be a "whole" learner, so education should be an embodied experience in all the ways possible; there is much the body remembers and knows, that the mind does not. In this way, the concept of education and what is educative would be a highly individualized one. For the punk learners in my research, the description of their perception of what was educative is specifically pertinent. Although their specific educational journeys were their own, it is likely that every learner has a journey that shapes their understanding of what education is and what is educative in their lives.

Simply put, the punk learners described themselves as learners from a very early age, albeit each perceived themselves as different types of learners, and not all descriptors were happy and engaging; a few participants did not find value in their learner self-concept. This learner self-concept originated from unknown sources, yet they were able to pinpoint experiences that led them to believe certain things about themselves.

The punk learners clearly identified their miseducative experiences. The majority of punk learners located their miseducation within their schooling, specifically with teachers or curriculum structures. Other punk learners were miseducated through engagement in a community that disappointed them in such a manner that felt traumatic. No matter the source, the miseducation impacted the learner self-concept and the desire to continue to learn, create, or be productive was stunted. A limitation of this analysis connects to the ways in which the majority of the punk learners identified as White males, which of course leads me to question the potential for the documented miseducative experiences to be particular to disenfranchised White male students. In other words, given the hegemonic structures of the schooling experience, the reality is that the miseducative experiences would have been of a completely different kind and type if, for instance, the punk learners identified with an othered population of students who had historically been marginalized or oppressed by schooling systems.

Given the depths of the learning process, we still do not fully understand; additional research into the ways in which learners perceive learning (rather than how we would like to measure outcomes of learning) may be helpful. As much as I am grateful for Olson's work on healing, I would like to acknowledge that there are gaps in her work that can be advanced by additional research into the lived experience of educative healing not isolated to school wounds. Table 5.12 showcases my interpretation of Olson's offerings related to healing, and how they can be used to advance further work in the discipline:

Additionally, there is much to explore as to further the concept that teachers can act as healers for students whose miseducation is deeply connected to their lived experiences, as students who are forced to navigate racist schooling structures (Duncan-Andrade, 2009; Ginwright, 2010).

Conclusion: A Desire Path

As I conclude my research analysis, I return to Mann's belief in education preventing the revenge and madness of humanity, as well as Dewey's assertion that education carries us through the dead spaces of our lives. These founding education theorists envisioned an educational system based on meeting the intellectual, as well as the emotional, needs of students; they knew that students could not be "made" to learn, rather teaching and learning was more of an "art" than a formula (Mann, 1840/1989).

In my research, the punk learners articulated the varied ways in which they were disconnected, alienated, or shamed during a miseducative

TABLE 5.12 Future Research in Educative Healing

Aims of Educative Healing	
Olson (2009)	Potential Further Research
Healing as to be able to survive schooling	Healing as to be able to confidently navigate all sites of learning
Healing as to re-engage in the institution of education	Healing as to contribute to chosen site of learning
Healing as to challenge the "old school culture" (202)	Healing as to re-create and re-imagine learning communities
Healing as a way to validate our learner "style"	Healing as to better understand ourselves as "do-ers" (Harrison, 2002)

experience; as educators, there is no doubt in our profession that there are ways in which students suffer in and outside of school. Yet, what remains only tacitly explored are the ways in which educators can be well-versed in coaching healing processes for learners to either create or reclaim a learner self-concept that, once wounded by miseducation, can be revived.

Public pedagogy can help us locate sites of empowered learning, social learning theory can assist us in understanding the role on interpersonal communication in learning, and self-directed learning theory can provide some pragmatic goals for learners to consider on their journey. But in order to fully actualize our inherent learning spirit, educators would need to be well-versed in the authentically educative, rather than the formal structures of what is considered educative, but is often miseducative. Additionally, if educators are to work with the miseducated learner, then attempts at education may be fruitless until educative healing has occurred. Educators, therefore, would be wise to understand the natures of educative healing before proceeding in any other vein.

With this professional trajectory in mind, I am drawn to the concept of the *desire path*. Desire paths are the "ultimate unbiased expression of natural human purpose and refer to tracks worn across grassy spaces, where people naturally walk—regardless of formal pathways" (Myhill, 2004). French phenomenologist Gaston Bachelard (1969) coined the term while referencing intentional footpaths as the "drawings we have lived" (p. 12). We see these desire paths (or desire lines as they are also referred) in parks, trails, greenways and other public spaces where there already exist as a concrete walkway of some sort; they occur when people travel their own way to meet their own goals, serve their own needs, and are often seen as important aspects of empowered human behavior:

> They are a means of deviancy and exploration—they chart new territory and open up paths to places that would otherwise be passed by. In all instances, desire lines are signs of a consensus that their way is worth walking; they are maintained only by the constant use of countless footsteps—without that, the lines fade and are forgotten. (Luckert, 2013, p. 318)

Speaking specifically in the sense of education research, the educative experience of learners can be seen as a desire path, on an individual scale, but with broader implications. For the punk learners in my research, engagement with punk served as an education desire path to reclaim or create a self-directed learner self-concept. If we as educators are to consider this perspective, the questions about and implications for education are many.

- How might we learn from learners' and their education desire paths as we construct and support sites of learning?
- How might educators become facilitators of learning in ways that encourage the educative experiences outside of schooling?
- How might we work to heal the miseducation that students and communities are currently suffering through?

Most importantly, if learners often create a desire path to experience the educative (or to heal) in order to become self-directed learners, what does this ultimately say about the education path that has been concreted? Perhaps our duty as educators is to dedicate our professional lives to consciously observing learners create their own educative desire paths, rather than force them to walk on the miseducative pavement.

In closing, I believe as scholars of education our profession demands a new era of scholarship where our focus is on the ways in which people are intuitive, naturally driven learners, as well as to explicate the already accessible, yet potentially disregarded, environments that nurture the inquiry and discovery necessary to fuel authentic education. If it is our aim in assisting our schooling system in honoring learning above all else, then our profession must be called to re-envision and imagine where new sites of learning already exist, so that we can nurture environments conducive to learning within all educational contexts. I believe, therefore, any new or improved system of education must be fueled and inspired by the essence of education that has often been marginalized. Given this, it is of the utmost importance that education scholars continue to remain experts on education, wherever it takes us.

References

Afro-Punk. (2007). *The movement*. Retrieved May 15, 2007, from http://www.afropunk.com/about_movement.html

Alvarado, J. (2012). Backyard brats and eastside punks. *Aztlan: A Journal of Chicano Studies, 37*(2), 157–180.

Andersen, M. (2004). *All the power: Revolution without illusion*. Chicago, IL: Punk Planet.

Anderson, T. (2012). *The experience of punk subcultural identity*. Unpublished doctoral dissertation, John F. Kennedy University.

Anderson, M., & Jenkins, M. (2003). *Dance of days*. Washington, DC: Soft Skull Press.

Ardizzone, L. (2005). Yelling and listening: Youth culture, punk, rock, and power. *Taboo: The Journal of Culture and Education*, 49–57.

Attfield, S. (2011). Punk rock and the value of auto-ethnographic writing about music. *Journal of Multidisciplinary International Studies, 8*(1).

Au, W. (Ed.). (2009). *Rethinking multicultural education*. Milwaukee, WI: Rethinking Schools.

Bachelard, G. (1969). *The poetics of reverie: Childhood, language, and the cosmos*, (D. Russell, Trans.). New York, NY: Orion Press.

Bag, A. (2011). *Violence girl: East L.A. rage to Hollywood stage: A chicana punk story*. Port Townsend, WA: Feral House.

Bag, A. (2014). We were there: Voices from L.A. punk's first wave. *Razorcake,* (79).

Barlie, N. (2014). How being punk rock makes me a better teacher. *Education Week*. Retrieved May 1, 2014, from http://www.edweek.org/tm/articles/2014/01/22/ctq_berile_punk.html

Barrett, D. (2013). DIY democracy: The direct action politics of US Punk collectives. *American Studies, 52*(2), 23–42.

Beer, D. (2014). *Punk sociology.* Basingstoke, England: Palgrave Macmillan.
Bennett, A. (2006). Punk's not dead: The continuing significance of punk rock for an older generation of fans. *Sociology, 40*(2), 219–235.
Biel, J. (2012). *Beyond the music: How punks are saving the world with DIY ethics, skills, and values.* Cleveland, OH: Microcosm.
Blush, S. (2010). *American hardcore: A tribal history.* Port Townsend WA: Feral House.
Bové, J., & Dufour, F. (2001). *The world is not for sale.* New York, NY: Verso.
BoySetsFire. (2000) After the eulogy. On *After the eulogy* (CD). Chicago, IL: Victory Records.
Bruner, J. S. (1996). *The culture of education.* Cambridge, MA: Harvard University Press.
Buchanan, R., & Fink, L. S. (2012). Zines in the classroom: Reading culture. *English Journal, 102*(2), 71–77.
Burdick, J., Sandlin, J., & O'Malley, M. (2013). *Problematizing public pedagogy.* New York, NY: Routledge.
Burkholder, Z. (2011). *Color in the classroom: How American schools taught race, 1900–1954.* New York, NY: Oxford University Press.
Butler, C.T., & McHenry, K. (2000). *Food not bombs.* Tucson, AZ: Sharp Press.
Cappo, R. (1988). No more [Youth of Today]. On *We're not in this alone* [CD]. New York, NY: Caroline Records
Caumont, A. (2003, February). Coloring outside the lines: A punk rock memoir. Book review. *Left Off The Dial.*
Cervenka. E., & Jocoy, J. (2002). *We're desperate: The punk rock photography of Jim Jocoy.* Brooklyn, NY: Powerhouse Books.
Cherry, E. (2006). Veganism as a cultural movement: A relational approach. *Social Movement Studies, 5*(2), 155–170.
Clark, D. (2004). The raw and the rotten: Punk cuisine. *Ethnology, 43*(1), 19–31.
Clark, D. (2013). The raw and the rotten: Punk cuisine. In C. Counihan & P. Van Esterik (Eds.) *Food and culture: A reader* (pp. 411–422). New York, NY: Routledge.
Coles, T. (2014). *Never mind the inspectors, here's punk learning.* Carmarthen, England: Independent Thinking Press.
Comstock, M. (2001). Grrrl zine networks: Re-composing spaces of authority, gender, and culture. *Journal of Advanced Composition, 21*(2), 384–409.
Cortes, C. (1979, April). The societal curriculum and the school curriculum: Allies or antagonists? *Association for the Supervision of Curriculum Development.*
Cortes, C. (1981). The societal curriculum: Implications for multiethnic education. In J.A. Banks (Ed.). *Education in the 80s: Multiethnic education* (pp. 24–32). Washington, DC: National Education Association.
Cowen, J. M., & Winters, M. A. (2013). Do charters retain teachers differently? Evidence from elementary schools in Florida. *Education, 8*(1), 14–42.
Cremin, L. (1976). *Public education.* New York, NY: Basic Books.

CrimethInc. Workers' Collective. (2001). *Days of war, nights of love: Crimethink for beginners*. Atlanta, GA: CrimethInc.

Crotty, M. (2004). *The foundations of social research* (3rd ed.). Thousand Oaks, CA: Sage.

Dale, P. (2012). *Anyone can do it: Empowerment, tradition and the punk underground: empowerment tradition and the punk underground*. Burlington, VT: Ashgate.

Dancis, B. (1978). Safety pins and class struggle: Punk rock and the left. *Socialist Review No. 39*, 8(3), 58–83.

Darder, A., Baltodano, M., & Torres, R. D. (Eds.). (2008). *The critical pedagogy reader* (2nd ed.). London, England: Routledge.

D'Angelica, C. (2009). *Beyond Bikini Kill: A history of Riot Grrl, from grrls to ladies.* ProQuest.

Davies, J. (1996, Spring). The future of "No Future": Punk rock and postmodern theory. *Journal of Popular Culture*, 29(4), 3.

Deegan, P. E. (2002). Recovery as a self-directed process of healing and transformation. *Occupational Therapy in Mental Health*, 17(3/4), 5–21.

Dewey, J. (1938/1997). *Experience and education*. New York, NY: Kappa Delta Pi.

Downes, J. (2012). The expansion of punk rock: Riot Grrrl challenges to gender power relations in British indie music subcultures. *Women's Studies*, 41(2), 204–237.

Dubar, P. (1986). No thanks [Uniform Choice]. On *Screaming for change* [LP]. Newport Beach, CA: WishingWell Records

Duncan-Andrade, J. M. (2009). Note to educators: Hope required when growing roses in concrete. *Harvard Educational Review*, 79(2), 181–194.

Duncombe, S., & Tremblay, M. (2011). *White riot: Punk rock and the politics of race*. New York, NY: Verso.

Dunn, K. (2008). Never mind the bollocks: The punk rock politics of global communication. *Review of International Studies*, 34, 193–210.

Eatough, V. & Smith, J. A. (2008). Interpretative phenomenological analysis. In C. Willig & W. Stainton Rogers (Eds.), *The Sage handbook of qualitatitive research in psychology*. London, England: Sage.

Eisner, E.W. (1994) *The educational imagination: On design and evaluation of school programs*, (3rd. ed.). New York, NY: Macmillan.

Ellsworth, E. (2005). *Places of learning: Media, architecture, pedagogy*. New York, NY: Routledge.

Emdin, C. (2010). *Urban science education for the hip-hop generation*. Rotterdam, the Netherlands: Sense.

England, Y. (2013). *A punk practice: The development of punk political activism, 1979–2004* (Doctoral dissertation). California State University, Chico, CA.

Ensminger, D. (2010). Redefining the body electric: Queering punk and hardcore. *Journal of Popular Music Studies*, 22(1), 50–67.

Ercoli, R. (2003). *Legends of punk: Photos from the vault*. San Francisco, CA: Manic D Press.

Fine, M. (1991). *Framing dropouts*. Albany, NY: State University of New York Press.

Fine, M., & Weiss, L. (2003). *Silenced voices and extraordinary conversations: Reimagining schools.* New York, NY: Teachers College Press.

Fiscella, A. (2012). From Muslim punks to taqwacore: An incomplete history of punk Islam. *Contemporary Islam, 6*(3), 255–281

Flores, H. (2006). *Food not lawns: How to turn your yard into a garden and your neighborhood into a community.* White River Junction, VT: Chelsea Green.

Forson, P. W., & Counihan, C. (Eds.). (2013). *Taking food public: Redefining foodways in a changing world.* London, England: Routledge.

Fox, D. (1983). Personal theories of teaching, *Studies in Higher Education and Teaching, 8*(2), 151–163.

Fox, D. (1983). Personal theories of teaching. *Studies in Higher Education, 8*(2), 151–164

Fox, K. J. (1987). Real punks and pretenders: The social organization of a counterculture. *Journal of Contemporary Ethnography, 16*(3), 344–370.

Freire, P. (1970). *Pedogogy of the oppressed.* New York, NY: Continuum.

Friesen, N., Henriksson, C., & Saevi, T. (2012). *Hermeneutic phenomenology in education: Method and practice.* New York, NY: Springer Science.

Garrett, B. T. (2011). *"We're the girls with the bad reputations": The rhetoric of Riot Grrrl.* (Doctoral dissertation). Western Carolina University, Cullowhee, NC.

Gatto, J. T. (2003). Against school. *Harper's Magazine, 307*(1840), 33.

Gatto, J. T. (2005). *Dumbing us down: The hidden curriculum of compulsory schooling.* Gabroila, British Columbia, Canada: Canada New Society Publishers.

Gay, G. (2000). *Culturally responsive teaching: Theory, research, & practice.* New York, NY: Teachers College Press.

Genette, G. (1983). *Narrative discourse: An essay in method.* Ithaca, NY: Cornell University Press.

George-Warren, H. (2007). *Punk 365* (365 Series). New York, NY: Harry N. Abrams.

Ginwright, S. (2010). *Black youth uprising: Activism & radical healing in urban America.* New York, NY: Teachers College Press.

Giroux, H. (2004a). Cultural studies, public pedagogy, and the responsibility of intellectuals. *Communication and Critical/Cultural Studies, 1*(1), 59–79.

Giroux, H. (2004b). Public pedagogy and the politics of neo-liberalism: Making the political more pedagogical. *Policy Futures in Education, 2*(3/4), 494–503.

Giroux, H. A. (2006, Fall). Higher education under siege: Implications for public intellectuals. *Thought & Action,* 63–78.

Giroux, H. A. (2009). Education and the crisis of youth: Schooling and the promise of democracy. *The Educational Forum, 73*(1), 8–18.

Goshert, J. C. (2000)."Punk" after the Pistols: American music, economics, and politics in the 1980s and 1990s. *Popular Music and Society, 24*(1), 85.

Griffin, N. (2012). Gendered performance and performing gender in the DIY punk and hardcore music scene. *Journal of International Women's Studies, 13*(2), 66–81.

Grow, G. (1991). Teaching learners to be self-directed. *Adult Education Quarterly, 41*(3) 125–149.

Haenfler, R. (2004). Rethinking subcultural resistance: Core values of the straight edge movement. *Journal of Contemporary Ethnography, 33*, 406.

Haenfler, R. (2006). *Straight edge: Clean living youth, hardcore punk, and social change.* New Brunswick, NJ: Rutgers University Press.

Hall, S. (1996). Cultural studies and its theoretical legacies. In D.Morley & K-H. Chen (Eds.), *Critical dialogues in cultural studies* (pp. 262–265). New York, NY: Routledge.

Hall, S., & Jefferson, T. (1976). *Resistance through rituals: Youth subcultures in postwar Britain.* London, England: Routledge.

Hancock, B. H., & . Lorr, M. J. (2012). More than just a soundtrack: Toward a technology of the collective in hardcore punk. *Journal of Contemporary Ethnography, 42,* 320.

Harper, M., & Cole, P. (2012). Member checking: Can benefits be gained similar to group therapy. *The Qualitative Report, 17*(2), 510–517.

Harrison, S. (2002). *The happy child: Changing the heart of education.* Boulder, CO: Sentient.

Hayes, E., & Gee, J. P. (2010). Public pedagogy in video games: Design, resources and affinity spaces. In J. A. Sandlin, B. D. Schultz, & J. Burdick (Eds.), *Handbook of public pedagogy* (pp. 185–193). New York, NY: Routledge.

Hearse, P. (1997, August). *Fighting racism and fascism in 1970s Britain: International news, 286.* Retrieved from https://www.greenleft.org.au/node/14066

Hebdige, D. (1979). *Subculture: The meaning of style.* London, England: Routledge.

Heidegger, M. (1927/1962). *Being and time* (J. Macquarrie & E. Robinson, Trans.). Oxford, England: Blackwell.

Heidegger, M. (1927/1982). *The basic problems of phenomenology* (A. Hofstadter, Trans.). Bloomington, IN: Indiana University Press.

Henderson, S. N. (2003). *Punk is political: The misunderstandings of an activist counterculture.* (Doctoral dissertation). University of Colorado, Denver.

Hern, M. (2008). *Everywhere all the time: A new deschooling reader.* Oakland, CA: AK Press.

Heynen, N. (2010). Cooking up non-violent civil-disobedient direct action for the hungry: 'Food not Bombs' and the resurgence of radical democracy in the US. *Urban Studies, 47*(6), 1225–1240.

Hill, M. L. (2007). *Beats, rhymes, and classroom life: Hip-hop pedagogy and the politics of identity.* New York, NY: Teachers College Press.

Hill, M. L. (2009). Wounded healing: Forming a storytelling community in hip-hop lit. *The Teachers College Record, 111*(1), 248–293.

Hill, M. L., & Petchauer, E. (Eds.). (2013). *Schooling hip-hop: Expanding hip-hop based education across the curriculum.* New York, NY: Teachers College Press.

Himelstein, A. (1998). *Tales of a punk rock nothing.* New Orleans, LA: New Mouth From the Dirty South.

Holt, J. (1964). *How children fail.* Brookfield, VT: Pitman.

Holt, J. (1976). *Instead of education: Ways to help people do things better.* Boulder, CO: Sentient.

Holt, J. (1989). *Learning all the time.* Boston, MA: Addison-Wesley. http://www.afropunk.com/about_movement.html

Huitt, W. (2001). Humanism and open education. *Educational Psychology Interactive.* Valdosta, GA: Valdosta State University. Retrieved November 10, 2006, from http://chiron.valdosta.edu/whuitt/col/affsys/humed.html

Husserl, E. (1913/1982). *Ideas pertaining to a pure phenomenology and to a phenomenological philosophy* (F. Kersten, Trans.). The Hague, the Netherlands: Nijhoff.

Hyland, N. E. (2005). Being a good teacher of black students? White teachers and unintentional racism. *Curriculum Inquiry, 35*(4), 429–459.

Illich, I. (1970). *Deschooling society: World Perspectives* (Vol. 44). New York, NY: Harper & Row.

Jackson, P. (1968/1990). *Life in classrooms.* New York, NY: Teachers College Press.

Jackson, S. L., Vann, W. F., Jr., Kotch, J. B., Pahel, B. T., & Lee, J. Y. (2011). Impact of poor oral health on children's school attendance and performance. *American Journal of Public Health, 101*(10), 1900.

Jeppesen, S. (2011). The DIY post-punk post-situationist politics of CrimethInc. *Anarchist Studies 19*(1), 23.

Jigsaw. (1991). *Jigsaw Youth Fanzine No. 4.* Olympia, WA: Jigsaw.

Johnson, S. (2011). *How can punk rock enlighten the education reform debate?* Retrieved from http://www.huffingtonpost.com/shaun-johnson/punk-rock-education-reform_b_861836.html

Kahn-Egan, S. (1998). Pedagogy of the pissed: Punk pedagogy in the first-year writing classroom. *College Composition and Communication, 49*(1), 99–104.

Kailin, J. (1994). Anti-racist staff development for teachers: Considerations of race, class and gender. *Teaching & Teacher Education, 10*(2), 169–184.

Kierkegaard, S. (1974). *Concluding unscientific postscript.* (D.F. Swenson & W. Lowrie, Trans.). Princeton, NJ: Princeton University Press.

Klein, N. (2000). *No logo.* New York, NY: Macmillan.

Knauss, C. (2009). Shut up and listen: Applied critical race theory in the classroom. *Race Ethnicity and Education, 12*(2), 133–154.

Kohl, H. (1991). *I won't learn from you! The role of assent in learning.* Minneapolis, MN: Milkweed Editions.

Kuhn, G. (Ed.). (2010). *Sober living for the revolution: Hardcore punk, straight edge, and radical politics.* Oakland, CA: PM Press.

Ladson-Billings, G. (1994). Who will teach our children? Preparing teachers to teach African American learners. In E. Hollins, J. King, & W. Hayman (Eds.), *Teaching diverse learners: Formulating a knowledge base for teaching diverse populations* (pp. 129–158). Albany, NY: State University of New York Press.

Ladson-Billings, G. (1995). Toward a theory of culturally relevant pedagogy. *American Educational Research Journal, 32,* 465–490.

Lahickey, B. (1997). *All ages: Reflections on straight edge*. Huntington Beach, CA: Revelation Books.

Laing, D. (1978, April). Interpreting punk rock. *Marxism Today*, 123.

Lawrence-Lightfoot, S. (2004). *The essential conversation: What parents and teachers can learn from each other*. New York, NY: Ballantine Books.

Leblanc, L. 1999. *Pretty in punk: Girls' gender resistance in a boys' subculture*. New Brunswick, NJ: Rutgers University Press.

Levine, H. G., & Stumpf, S. H. (1983). Statements of fear through cultural symbols: Punk rock as a reflective subculture. *Youth & Society, 14*(4), 417–435.

Lewis, A. (2001). There is no "race" in the schoolyard: Color-blind ideology in an (almost) all-White school. *American Educational Research Journal, 38*(4), 781–811.

Luckert, E. (2012). Drawings we have lived: Mapping desire lines in Edmonton. *Constellations, 4*(1), 318–327.

MacKaye, I. (1981) *Straight edge: Minor Threat first demo tape* [CD]. Washington, DC: Dischord Records.

Mageary, J. (2012). *"Rise above/we're gonna rise above": A qualitative inquiry into the use of hardcore culture as context for the development of preferred identities*. ProQuest, 247.

Malott, C., & Peña, M. (2004). *Punk rockers' revolution: A pedagogy of race, class, and gender* (Vol. 223). New York, NY: Peter Lang.

Mann, H. (1840/1989). *On the art of teaching*. Carlisle, MA: Applewood Books.

Marcus, S. (2010). *Girls to the front: The true story of the Riot Grrrl movement*. New York, NY: HarperCollins.

Marsh, C. J., & Willis, G. (2003). *Curriculum: Alternative approaches, ongoing issues* (3rd ed.). Upper Saddle River, NJ: Merrill Prentice Hall.

McDonald, J. R. (1987). Suicidal rage: An analysis of hardcore punk lyrics. *Popular Music & Society, 11*(3), 91–102.

McHenry, K. (2012). *Hungry for peace*. Tucson, AZ: See Sharp Press

McLaren, P. (2014). *Life in schools: An introduction to critical pedagogy in the foundations of education* (6th ed.). Boulder, CO: Paradigm.

McLaren, P., & Kincheloe, J. L. (Eds.). (2007). *Critical pedagogy: Where are we now?* (Vol. 299). New York, NY: Peter Lang.

McNeil, D. (2004). Afropunk: The rock 'n'roll nigger experience: Making up reality—race, rock, and wrestling. *Bright Lights Film Journal, 44*.

McWhirter, E. H., Ramos, K., & Medina, C. (2013). ¿Y ahora qué? Anticipated immigration status barriers and Latina/o high school students' future expectations. *Cultural Diversity and Ethnic Minority Psychology, 19*(3), 288.

Mercer, S. (2011). *Towards an understanding of language learner self-concept* (Vol. 12). Springer Science & Business Media.

Milner, H. R. (2013). Analyzing poverty, learning, and teaching through a critical race theory lens. *Review of Research in Education, 37*(1), 1–53.

Monem, N. (2007) *Riot Grrrl: Revolution girl style now!*, London, England: Black Dog.

Moore, R. (2007). Friends don't let friends listen to corporate rock: Punk as a field of cultural production. *Journal of Contemporary Ethnography 36*, 438–474.

Moore, R. (2010). *Sells like teen spirit: Music, youth culture, and social crisis.* New York, NY: New York University Press.

Moore, R., & Roberts, M. (2009). Do-it-yourself mobilization: Punk and social movements. *Mobilization, 14*(3), 273–291.

Moran, I. (2011). Punk: The do-it-yourself subculture. *Social Sciences Journal, 10*(1), 1–8.

Morrell, E., & Duncan-Andrade, J. (2002). Toward a critical classroom discourse: Promoting academic literacy through engaging hip-hop culture with urban youth. *English Journal, 91*(6), 88–94.

Moskowitz, I. C. (2005). *Vegan with a vengeance: Over 150 delicious, cheap, animal-free recipes that rock.* Boston, MA: Da Capo Press.

Myhill, C. (2004). Commercial success by looking for desire lines. In M. Masoodian, S. Jones, & B. Rogers (Eds.), *Proceedings of 6th Asia Pacific Computer-Human Interaction Conference.* Berlin, Germany: Springer.

Nguyen, M. (1998, November/December). It's (not) a White world: Looking for race in punk. *Punk Planet.*

Nieto, S. (1994). Affirmation, solidarity, & critique: Moving beyond tolerance in multicultural education. *Multicultural Education, 1*(4), 9–38.

Nieto, S., & Bode, P. (2007). *Affirming diversity: The sociopolitical context of multicultural education.* Columbus, OH: Pearson.

Noddings, N. (2003). *Happiness and education.* Cambridge, England: Cambridge University Press.

Nomous, O. (2007, June). Race, anarchy, and punk rock: The impact of cultural boundaries within the anarchist movement. *Illvox: Anarchist people of color, race, anarchy, revolution.* Retrieved May 1, 2009, from http://illvox.org/2007

O'Connor, A. (2003). Punk subculture in Mexico and the anti-globalization movement: A report from the front. *New Political Science, 25*(1), 43–53.

O'Hara, C. (1999). *The philosophy of punk: More than noise.* Oakland, CA: AK Press.

O'Malley, M. P., Sandlin, J., & Burdick, J. (2010). *Public pedagogy. The encyclopedia of curriculum studies.* Thousand Oaks, CA: Sage.

Olson, K. (2009). *Wounded by school: Recapturing the joy in learning and standing up to old school culture.* New York, NY: Teachers College Press.

One, O. (2005). Punk power in the first-year writing classroom. *Teaching English in the Two-Year College, 32*(4), 358–369.

Ott, J. (2000). *My world: Ramblings of an aging gutter punk.* Berkeley, CA: Hopeless Records.

Patton, M. Q. (2002). *Qualitative research & evaluation methods.* Thousand Oaks, CA: Sage.

Pearson, J. (2004). Coffin nails [The Locus]. On *Follow the flock, Step in shit* [EP]. San Diego, CA: Three One G Records.

People for the Ethical Treatment of Animals (PETA). (2009). Retrieved from http://www.peta2.com/heroes/the-locust

Peterson, B. (2009). *Burning fight: The nineties hardcore revolution in ethics, politics, spirit and sound.* Huntington Beach, CA: Revelation Records.

Peterson, R., & Bennett, A. (2004). *Music scenes: Local, translocal and virtual.* Nashville, TN: Vanderbilt University Press.

Pfeiffer, D. A. (2006). *Eating fossil fuels: Oil, food and the coming crisis in agriculture.* Gabriola Island, British Columbia, Canada: New Society.

Pinar, W. (2010a). Foreword. In J. A. Sandlin, B. D. Schultz, & J. Burdick (Eds.), *Handbook of public pedagogy* (pp. xv–xix). New York, NY: Routledge.

Pinar, W. (2012). *What is curriculum theory?* New York, NY: Routledge.

Polletta, F. (1999). Free spaces in collective action. *Theory Into Action, 28,* 1–38.

Porcelly, J. (1987). Where it ends [Project X]. *On Project X* [LP]. New York, NY: Schism Records

Portwood-Stacer, L. (2012). Anti-consumption as tactical resistance: Anarchists, subculture, and activist strategy. *Journal of Consumer Culture, 12*(1), 87–105.

Postman, N. (1995). *The end of education: Redefining the value of school.* New York, NY: Vintage Books.

Postman, N., & Weingartner, C. (1971). *Teaching as a subversive activity.* New York, NY: Delta.

Propaghandi. (1996). Nailing Descartes to the wall/(liquid) meat is still murder. In *Less Talk, More Rock* [CD]. San Francisco, CA: Fat Wreck Chords.

Powley, E. H., & Piderit, S. K. (2008). Tending wounds elements of the organizational healing process. *The Journal of Applied Behavioral Science, 44*(1), 134–149.

Purchla, J. (2011). The powers that be: Processes of control in 'crew scene hardcore.' *Ethnography, 12*(2), 198–223.

Ramírez-Sánchez, R. (2008). Marginalization from within: Expanding co-cultural theory through the experience of the Afro-Punk. *The Howard Journal of Communications, 19*(2), 89–104.

Razorcake (Eds.). (2007). *Razorcake* (Vol. 40). Los Angeles, CA: Razorcake.

Razorcake (Eds.). (2010). *Razorcake* (Vol. 57). Los Angeles, CA: Razorcake.

Reddington, H. (2007). *The lost women of rock music: Female musicians of the punk era.* Burlington, VT: Ashgate.

Rich, A. (1986). *Blood, bread, and poetry.* New York, NY: Norton.

Rohrer, I. (2014). *Cohesion and dissolution: Friendship in the globalized punk and hardcore scene of Buenos Aires.* Berlin, Germany: Springer VS.

Roman, L. G. (1987). *Punk femininity: The formation of young women's gender identities and class relations within the extramural curriculum of a contemporary subculture.* (Doctoral dissertation). University of Wisconsin, Madison, WI.

Ronfeldt, M., Loeb, S., & Wyckoff, J. (2013). How teacher turnover harms student achievement. *American Educational Research Journal, 50*(1), 4–36.

Rosenberg, J., & Garofalo, G. (1998). Riot Grrrl: Revolutions from within. *Signs, 23*(3), 809–841.

Rury, J. (2005). *Urban education in the United States: A historical reader.* London, England: Palgrave Macmillan.

Sabin, R. (1999). *Punk rock. So what?: The cultural legacy of punk.* London, England: Routledge.

Sandlin, J. A., & Milam, J. (2008). Mixing pop (culture) and politics: Cultural resistance, culture jamming, and anti-consumption activism as critical public pedagogy. *Curriculum Inquiry, 38*(3), 323–349.

Sandlin, J. A., Schultz, B. D., & Burdick, J. (2010). *Handbook of public pedagogy.* New York, NY: Routledge.

Schill, B. J. (2012). Nothing is permitted anymore: Postanarchism, gnosticism, and the end of production. *Anarchist Studies, 20*(1).

Schilt, K., & Zobl, E. (2008). Connecting the dots. In A. Harris (Ed.). *New wave cultures: Feminism, sub-cultures and activism* (pp. 171–192). New York, NY: Routledge.

Schlosser, E. (2001). *Fast food nation: The dark side of the all-American meal.* Boston, MA: Houghton Mifflin Harcourt.

Schneider, M. (2002, November). Do school facilities affect academic outcomes? *National Clearinghouse for Educational Facilities.* Retrieved from http://www.ncef.org/pubs/outcomes.pdf

Schubert, W. H. (1981). Knowledge about out-of-school curriculum. *Educational Forum, 45*, 185–199.

Schubert, W. H. (2010). Outside curricula and public pedagogy. In J. A. Sandlin, B. D. Schultz, & J. Burdick (Eds.), *Handbook of public pedagogy* (pp. 10–19). New York, NY: Routledge.

Scott-Dixon, K. (1999). Ezines and feminist activism: Building a community. *Resources for Feminist Research, 27*(1/2), 127.

Seconds, K (1984). Straight on [7 Seconds]. *On the Crew* [CD]. Los Angeles, CA: BYO Records.

Seidl, B. (2007). Working with communities to explore and personalize culturally relevant pedagogies push, double images, and raced talk. *Journal of Teacher Education, 58*(2), 168–183.

Seidman, I. (2006). *Interviewing as qualitative research.* New York, NY: Teachers College Press.

Seidman, I. (2013). *Interviewing as qualitative research: A guide for researchers in education and the social sciences.* New York, NY: Teachers College Press.

Shahan, C. M. (2013). *Punk rock and German crisis: Adaptation and resistance after 1977.* New York, NY: Palgrave Macmillan.

Shermer, T. (2004, May). Black invisibility and racism in punk rock. *HipMama.*

Shor, I. (1987). *Critical teaching and everyday life.* Boston, MA: South End Press.

Shor, I. (1996). *When students have power: Negotiating authority in a critical pedagogy.* Chicago, IL: University of Chicago Press.

Simon, B. S. (1997). Entering the pit: Slam dancing and modernity. *The Journal of Popular Culture, 31*(1), 149–176.

Sirc, G. (1997). Never mind the tagmemics, Where's the Sex Pistols? *College Composition and Communication, 48*(1), 9–29.

Sleeter, C. E. (2000). Creating an empowering multicultural curriculum. *Race, Gender & Class,* 178–196.

Smith, J. A. (1996). Beyond the divide between cognition and discourse: Using interpretative phenomenological analysis in health psychology. *Psychology and Health, 11*(2), 261–271.

Smith, J. A., & Osborn, M. (2003) Interpretative phenomenological analysis. In J. A. Smith (Ed.), *Qualitative psychology: A practical guide to methods.* Thousand Oaks, CA: Sage.

Smith, J. A., Flowers, P., & Larkin, M. (2009). *Interpretive phenomenological analysis: Theory, method and research.* Los Angeles, CA: Sage.

Soep, E., & Chavez, V. (2010). *Drop that knowledge: Youth radio stories.* Los Angeles, CA: University of California Press.

Spring, J. (2012a). *Deculturalization and the struggle for equality: A brief history of the education of dominated cultures in the United States.* New York, NY: McGraw-Hill.

Spring, J. (2012b). *The American school 1642–2001.* New York, NY: McGraw-Hill.

Sprouse, M. (1990). *Threat by example.* San Francisco, CA: Pressure Drop Press.

Spurlock, M. (2004). *Super size me: A film of epic proportions* [DVD video].

Stockburger, I. Z. (2011) *Making zines, making selves: Identity construction in DIY autobiography.* ProQuest, 232.

Strong, C. (2011). Grunge, Riot Grrrl and the forgetting of women in popular culture. *The Journal of Popular Culture, 44*(2), 398–416.

The Locust. (2004). Coffin nails. On *Follow the Flock* [CD].

Thompson, A. (2010). *From bad brains to Afro-punk: An analysis of identity, consciousness, and liberation through punk rock from 1977–2010* (Unpublished doctoral dissertation, Cornell University, Ithaca, NY.

Thompson, S. (2004). Crass commodities. *Popular Music and Society, 27*(3), 307–322.

Traber, D. S. (2001) LA's "White minority": Punk and the contradictions of self-marginalization. *Cultural Critique, 48,* 30–64.

Traber, D. S. (2007). *Whiteness, otherness, and the individualism paradox from huck to punk.* New York, NY: Palgrave Macmillan.

Tyack, D. (1974). *The one best system: The history of American urban education.* Boston, MA: Harvard University Press.

Uline, C., & Tschannen-Moran, M. (2008). The walls speak: The interplay of quality facilities, school climate, and student achievement. *Journal of Educational Administration, 46*(1), 55–73.

Valenzuela, A. (1999). *Subtractive schooling: US-Mexican youth and the politics of caring.* New York, NY: Suny Press.

Van Manen, M. (1990). *Researching lived experience: Human science for an action sensitive pedagogy* (2nd ed.). New York, NY: State University of New York Press.
Van Manen, M. (1995). On the epistemology of reflective practice. *Teachers and teaching: Theory and practice, 1*(1), 33–50.
Ventegodt, S., Andersen, N. J., & Merrick, J. (2003). Holistic medicine III: The holistic process theory of healing. *The Scientific World Journal, 3,* 1138–1146.
Vygotsky, L. S. (1978). *Mind in society.* Cambridge, MA: Harvard University Press.
Vygotsky, L.V. (1997). *Educational psychology.* Boca Raton, FL: Fort Lucie Press.
Wald, G., & Gottlieb, J. (1993). Smells like teen spirit: Riot Grrrls, revolution, and women in independent rock. *Critical Matrix: The Princeton Journal of Women, Gender, and Culture, 7,* 2.
Wan, A. (1999). Not just for kids anymore: Using zines in the classroom. *The Radical Teacher, 55,* 15–19.
Ward, J. J. (1996). "This is Germany! It's 1933!" Appropriations and constructions of "fascism" in New York punk/hardcore in the 1980s. *The Journal of Popular Culture, 30*(3), 155–184.
Ware, E., Ahern, S., Elovaara, M., Erbe, M., Varas-Diaz, N., Rivera-Segarra, E.,... & Fellezs, K. (2014). *Hardcore, punk, and other junk: Aggressive sounds in contemporary music.* E. J. Abbey, & C. Helb (Eds.). New York, NY: Lexington Books.
Wertsch, J. A (Ed.). (1981). *The concept of activity in Soviet psychology* (pp. 144–188). New York, NY: Sharpe.
Wertsch, J. A. (1985). *Vygotsky and the social formation of mind.* Cambridge, MA: Harvard University Press.
Willis, S. (1993, Winter). Hardcore: Subculture American style. *Critical Inquiry, 19*(2), 365–383.
Wink, J. (2005). *Critical pedagogy: Notes from the real world.* Boston, MA: Pearson.
Wood, R. T. (2006). *Straightedge youth: Complexity and contradictions of a subculture.* New York, NY: Syracuse University Press.
Zinn, H. (2000). Preface. In C. T. Butler & K. McHenry, *Food not bombs.* Tucson, AZ: See Sharp Press.
Zobl, E. (2001). Stop sexism with style! Grrrl: Rebel. An interview with the Carol and Elise. In *Grrrlzines.net.* Retrieved July 9, 2009, from http://grrrlzines.net/interviews/grrrlrebel.htm
Zobl, E. (2004a). Personality liberation front: Exploring feminism and punk at its best. An interview with Kylie Lewis. In *Grrrlzines.net.* Retrieved July 8, 2009, from http://www.grrrlzines.net/interviews/personalityliberation.htm
Zobl, E. (2004b). The power of pen publishing: International grrrl zines and distros. *Feminist Collections, 26*(1), 20–24.
Zobl, E. (2004c). Revolution grrrl and lady style, now! *Peach Review 16*(4), 445–452.
Zobl, E. (2004d). Persephone is pissed!: Grrl zine reading, making and distributing across the globe. *Hecate, 30*(2), 156–175.

Zobl, E. (2009). Cultural production, transnational networking, and critical reflection in feminist 'zines. *Signs, 35*(1), 1–12.

Additional Resources

Anonymous. 2001. *Evasion.* Atlanta, GA: CrimethInc.

Bail, K. (Ed.). (1996). *DIY feminism.* Sydney, Australia: Allen & Unwin.

Belsito, P., & Davis, B. (1983). *Hardcore California: A history of punk and new wave.* San Francisco, CA: Last Gasp.

Bjerede, M. (2012). *DIY learning: Schoolers, edupunks, and makers challenge education as we know it.* Retreived from http://radar.oreilly.com/2012/05/schoolers-edupunks-makers-learning.html

Bruner, J. S. (1960/1977). *The process of education.* Cambridge, MA: Harvard University Press.

Buchanan, R. J. (2009). *Zine narratives: Subjectivities and stories of five influential zine creators.* ProQuest, 247.

Caldwell, A. (2011). Will tweet for food: Microblogging mobile food trucks—online, offline and in line. In P. W. Forson & C. Counihan, (Eds.), *Taking food public: Redefining foodways in a changing world.* London, England: Routledge.

Cogan, B. (2006). *The encyclopedia of punk music and culture.* Westport, CT: Greenwood Press.

Duncan-Andrade, J. M., & Morrell, E. (2008). *The art of critical pedagogy.* New York, NY: Peter Lang.

Frey, H. (2003, January 13). Kathleen Hanna's fire. *The Nation.*

Frith, S. (1978). The punk bohemians. *New Society, 43*(805), 535–536.

Gee, J. P. (2004). *Situated language and learning: A critique of traditional schooling.* New York, NY: Routledge.

Giroux, H. A., & Simon, R. I. (1988). Schooling, popular culture, and a pedagogy of possibility. *Journal of Education, 170*(1), 9–26.

Jenlink, P. M. (2005). Editorial: Public pedagogy and the intellectual work of teachers. *Teacher Education and Practice, 18,* 252–264.

Kearney, M. C. (2006). *Girls make media.* New York, NY: Routledge.

Lamy, P., & Levin, J. (1985). Punk and middle class values: A content analysis. *Youth and Society, 17*(2), 157–170.

Lull, J. (1987). Thrashing in the pit: An ethnography of San Francisco punk subculture. In T.R. Lindlof (Ed.), *Natural audiences: Qualitative research of media use and its effects* (pp. 225–252). Norwood, NJ: Ablex.

MacKaye, I. (1983). *Out of step: Minor Threat.* On *Out of step* [CD]. Washington, DC: Dischord Records.

Maskell, S. (2009). Performing punk: Bad brains and the construction of identity. *Journal of Popular Music Studies, 21*(4), 411–426.

Mayo, P. (2003). A rationale for a transformative approach to education. *Journal of Transformative Education, 1,* 38–57.

McNeil, L., & McCain, G. (2006). *Please kill me: The uncensored oral history of punk*. New York, NY: Grove Press.

Milenkovic, D. (2007). The subcultural group of hardcore punk: Sociological research of the group members' social origin and their attitudes to nation, religion and the consumer society values. *Facta Universitatis: Series Philosophy and Sociology, 6*(1), 67–80.

Papanek, V. (2010). The future isn't what it used to be. *Design Issues, 5*(1) 4–17.

Pinar, W. (2010b). On the privacy of public pedagogy. In J. A. Sandlin, B. D. Schultz, & J. Burdick (Eds.), *Handbook of public pedagogy* (pp. 45–55). New York, NY: Routledge.

Reisberg, J. (2009, April). Count me out: A qualitative-phenomenological inquiry into the experience of being a male in the American hardcore music scene. *The Official Journal of the Confluence Undergraduate Humanistic Psychology Alliance.*

Roman, L. G. (1993). Double exposure: The politics of feminist materialist ethnography. *Educational Theory, 43*(3), 279–308.

Shahan, C. (2011). The sounds of terror: Punk, post-punk and the RAF after 1977. *Popular Music and Society, 34*(3), 369–386.

Shepard, B., & Hayduk, R. (Eds.). (2002). *From ACT UP to the WTO: Urban protest and community building in the era of globalization*. New York, NY: Verso.

Slander. (2000). *Beyond the screams/mas alla los gritos*. Retrieved May 15, 2009, from http://www.worsethanqueer.com/slander/pp37.html

Smith, G. (2011). White mutants of straight edge: The avant-garde of abstinence. *The Journal of Popular Culture, 44*(3), 633–646.

Spooner, J. (Producer). (2003). *Afro-punk* [Motion picture]. Retrieved from www.afropunk.com

Upski Wimsatt, W. (1999). *No more prisons: Urban life, homeschooling, hip-hop leadership, the cool rich kids movement, a hitchhiker's guide to community organizing, and why philanthropy is the greatest art form of the 21st century*. New York, NY: Soft Skull Press.

Van Manen, M. (2012). *The heuristic reduction: Wonder*. Retrieved January 5, 2012, from: www.phenomenologyonline.com/inquiry/11.html

Vygotsky, L. S. (1981). The genesis of higher mental functions (J. V. Wertsch, Trans) In J V Wertsch, *The concept of activity in Soviet psychology*. Armonk, NY: Sharpe.

Weber, M. C. (2004). Walking on the edge: A phenomenology of the straight edge music subculture. (Master's thesis). Retrieved from ProQuest (1424370).

Widdicombe, S., & Wooffitt, R. (1990). 'Being' versus 'doing' punk: On achieving authenticity as a member. *Journal of Language and Social Psychology, 9*, 257–277.

Widdicombe, S., & Wooffitt, R. (1995). *The language of youth subcultures: Social identity in action*. London, England: Harvester Wheatsheaf.

Willis, P. (1977). *Learning to labor: How working class kids get working class jobs*. New York, NY: Columbia University Press.

Willis, P. (1978). *Profane culture.* London, England: Routledge.
Willis, P. (1990). *Common culture: Symbolic work at play in the everyday cultures of the young.* Boulder, CO: Westview.
Zinn, H. (2011). *A young people's history of the United States: Columbus to the war on terror.* New York, NY: Seven Stories Press.

Made in the USA
Columbia, SC
26 October 2020